MW00387436

GOOD LUCK DON'T SUCK

A TACTICAL GUIDE TO EARLY SUCCESS IN THE WORKPLACE

Good Luck,
Don't Suck

Kevin Long

Copyright 2020 by GLDS Consulting Group, LLC

ISBN 978-1-7346795-1-9 (hardcover)
ISBN 978-1-7346795-2-6 (e-book)
ISBN 978-1-7346795-0-2 (paperback)

Printed in the United States of America

Cover Designed by Wilson Piechazek
Photo by Caroline Jok

The opinions expressed are those of the authors and do not
reflect those of the U.S. Air Force, the Department of Defense
or the U.S. Government.

While the author has made every effort to provide accurate
Telephone numbers, Internet addresses, and other contact
information at the time of publication, neither the publisher nor
the author assumes any responsibility for errors, or for changes
that occur after publication. Further, the publisher does not
have any control over and does not assume any responsibility
for author or third-party websites or their content.

To Alicia, Jay, and Ashley for allowing us to be fully into this crazy endeavor and supporting us in helping people not suck.

Managers light a fire under people;
leaders light a fire in people.
- Kathy Austin

Introduction

We are passionate about making people a better version of themselves. We believe that the same actions that make you successful in the workplace can be applied to all aspects of life. We aim to collect those actions and deliver them to you, the reader.

We first met within an Air Force affiliated collegiate, professional development organization; think of it as a professional co-ed fraternity. This student-run organization selects and utilizes high-performing alumni to serve as mentors to its national leadership team. We all graduated, moved on, and were selected into these alumni mentor roles and, between the three of us, have served as these leadership consultants for a combined 23 years. We have affected the lives of thousands, both students and soon to be Air Force officers. We used this forum not only to hone the students' talents but also our own. Our day job remains as Air Force officers, supporting and defending the Constitution of our great nation. We found quick success in our careers, Kevin as an A-10 pilot, Gabbe as an Aircraft Maintenance Officer, and Dan as an Acquisition Professional. As we looked around at our peers, both in and out of uniform, we saw a significant amount of unlocked potential to excel. This potential remained chained not due to a lack of intelligence, motivation, or technical skills, but mostly because no one ever gave them the tactical tips on how to become a high performer.

Now you may be thinking; there are hundreds of books on how to be successful, written by powerful, sometimes heroic, CEOs, presidents, and generals. You are right--there are. We have read quite a variety of them and are huge fans of many. So, what makes *The Tactical Guide to Early Success* any different? We are not going to tell you how to create a vision for a large team, we are not going to talk about large-scale organizational change, and we are not going to talk about what you need to do to be the next Jeff Bezos. The point of this book is not for you to learn about all the great ideas that you will need in fifteen years when you are running the show with more gray hair (or no hair at all). This book is about the here and now. We want to provide you with on-the-job tactics that you can employ on Monday morning that will make you a successful employee, leader, and influencer in your workplace regardless of your position.

We have spent the last two years developing industry-agnostic Tactics, Techniques, and Procedures (TTPs) to help start your career on the right foot or launch your existing career on a different trajectory. These were developed not only through our experiences in world-class training programs hosted by the Department of Defense but also through listening to our mentors and analyzing our own habits (for better or worse), communication techniques, personal relationships, and more. All of this to bring you a no holds barred assessment of what we have done well, what we have totally botched, what we are currently doing, and what our plans are for continued success in the future. The book will take you on a journey to learn more about this, but the bottom line is being successful later in life is much easier if you get started now!

A major difference that this book brings to the audience is that we are both generationally the same as the audience and come from normal pedigree. You will not find outdated examples of how the workplace functions, we will not reference Vietnam, and pagers were basically non-existent in our lives. We do not have any tales of Harvard or other top-tier universities, and this is not some wordy philosophy book that tip-toes around the meaning of leadership. We have practiced what we have preached. Some of today's most prevalent leadership philosophers – Sinek, Maxwell, and Robins –

are indeed experts in the leadership field, but we have been down working in the field. We are products of the lessons written in this book. It has worked for us, just as it will work for you. If you walk away with any knowledge on how to be a better, more influential, or more productive leader, then the hard work in creating this book will have been worth it.

Leading. When we think of the word, most people instinctively think of influencing, and possibly managing, those around you. The premise of this book is that success is dependent on the amount of *influence* you have within your office. One of this book's foundational beliefs is that influence and leadership are tightly correlated.

Managing. Put that action in your back pocket and try to think of it as little as possible while reading this book. Instead, focus more on leading by influencing. Managing is a different skill set that while a useful tool, is not the focus of this book. You may not be a supervisor, team leader, or even a subject matter expert (fun fact: Other than general leadership philosophy and building PowerPoints, the three of us have never been the expert at anything), but if you can influence what is happening at the office, you are leading. So, when you read leading in this book, think influencing, when you read influencing, think leading.

Now when thinking of leading, you probably envision leading subordinates, people that report to you, and work directly under you. Let us twist that for you. Believe it or not, leading is not a single downward direction but instead has four different vectors to which it can be applied. This book will explore each: **Leading Self**; **Leading Up**; **Leading Across**; and **Leading Down**. This book is organized by each of those areas – areas that you can influence. You may realize that not all sections of the book apply to you right now as you may not have subordinates, or you may be one of the brave that do not have a boss (although finding someone who does not have a boss of some sort is tough) - that is okay! You will still be able to arm yourself with useful chunks of knowledge you pull from those sections to use at a future date or share with someone who comes to you for assistance. If you look through the table of contents and see a section you want to immediately jump to, go for it. We have built this book in this particular fashion so you can reference the material quickly (hence the title "Tactical Guide") so you do not waste time thumbing through pages looking for what pertains to you.

Earlier in the introduction, we mentioned the term TTPs. TTP is a term used throughout the military to describe best practices that have been proven true through military use in wartime or exercise. TTPs tell military operators how to maximize the capability of existing personnel, equipment, and supporting resources. They also describe how to use a plane, or rifle, or movement, in a way you had never thought of before. Airmen depend on these to perfect the craft of defending ground forces and striking targets deep in enemy territory. Soldiers use TTPs to expertly overwhelm an enemy force on the battlefield, or more commonly now, storm a building. Sailors use TTPs to protect our economic sea lanes and project America's power to shores near and far. The Marines use TTPs to storm beaches, kick down doors, and, honestly, do America's dirty work. *The Tactical Guide to Early Success* will extract those TTPs that will allow you to go into work tomorrow and simply perform better than you did today. TTPs from outside of the military may be seen as best practices in the day-to-day job or tricks of the trade around any type of workplace. One of the main things to know about these tactical tips is that they should be plug and play wherever you find yourself working. We highlight these as **Tactical Tips** throughout the text and compile them at the end for quick reference.

Through our research, we could not find a great example of how to write a nonfiction book from three different perspectives. We opted instead to make it a little easier on you. Throughout the book, we will share our own experiences from a singular perspective so you do not need to worry if it is Dan, Gabbe, or Kevin telling the story.

You probably are still scratching your head about the title, Good Luck, Don't Suck. It seems a bit brash and vague. As we have mentored students, we ended every conversation the same way, with this simple line. It is to serve as a reminder that sometimes success is dependent on more than just hard work and preparation. Luck is defined in the dictionary as "success or failure apparently brought by chance rather than through one's own action." While we agree that sometimes things are out of your control, we would like to think that good luck is where preparation meets opportunity. That does not happen every day, so when it does, don't blow it! **Good Luck, Don't Suck.**

*Successful people do what unsuccessful people
are not willing to do. Don't wish it were easier; wish
you were better.*
- Jim Rohn

Overarching Themes
for Success

There are a few topics that apply to every direction of influencing:
Defining Success, Ownership, Trust, and Getting past "No." These
are introduced briefly here, but bits and pieces of these lessons
are presented throughout the book.

Definition of Success

You may have heard the phrase "Success Begets Success"; I like to think of it as the snowball theory, once your success builds momentum, it grows quickly and is difficult to slow down. For example, many times, hiring authorities leverage someone else's opinion on how good someone is. You went to Harvard? You must be special! You were the president of a fraternity? You must be a leader! You were chosen as a Rhodes Scholar? You must have potential! You were hired by Google? You must be a tech genius! You get the pattern. In our view, people trust other people's opinions of you possibly more than they believe their own opinion after a first impression.

There are good and bad sides to this snowball theory. If you do not find the spark that kickstarts your momentum, you could be frustrated by others whose "snowball" has already started getting the jobs and promotions that you want and, possibly, deserve. However, if you stay the course, keep grinding, and dedicate yourself to perfecting your skillset within your field, your time will come, and you will find success.

Success is many times sought after, and, more often than not, it is left unclaimed. A mistake people make early on is not clearly defining their personal success and what it truly means to them. So, what defines success? Success in basic terms means accomplishing something with aim or purpose. This definition is very general, but success is going to be different to everyone, and there is also going to be different levels and scope of success. It can be something as little as changing the oil in a car, launching a website, or taking over a company you have worked at for years. The magnitudes will vary, for success is not so much the whole "being" successful but rather the "how" to get there.

Success is not black and white. As previously mentioned, it can be applied in many different ways. Some people define it by money, some by love, some by fame, and some by the people they surround themselves with. Success is both a factual and emotional feeling. Literally speaking, accomplishing any task technically makes you successful, but does completing a small, simple, task make you feel successful? Success takes an emotional role as well. You can feel successful even without completing something 100%, and you can also crush something and not feel wholly satisfied. To build your definition of success you need to think about what your end state is. You need to think about how you want your life to be like. Once you have the end in mind you need to visualize how you can break that end state into goals. Realize that along the way you may need to adapt those goals, but most importantly, you must be ready to crush the goals you set.

What are your goals? Write them down and make them measurable. Know that you, almost certainly, will fail along the way. One of my mentors, Major General (retired) Al Flowers, has a saying, "If you have never failed, I would be interested in seeing what you have achieved." A significant point to tie into success, which some people tend to forget about, is that success many times comes after having failed. When Edison invented the light bulb, he also learned 999 ways how not to make a lightbulb. Failures can undoubtedly be distracting and discouraging. Getting too caught up in those failures can detract from success. Do not loom on the failure. Instead, analyze what happened, pull the lessons learned from your experience, grow from it, and move forward. This is where adapting goals comes in. How you define success will change for you, and that is okay. You will adapt over time with life milestones and personal development, and it only makes sense that your aim and purpose will adapt alongside you.

Adapting goals seemed like something I would only do in moderation. Little did I know the word *adapt* would actually end up meaning a complete overhaul. My goals were to be a four-star general or at least a successful maintenance officer. This goal would have been easy for a single person, no spouse, and no kiddos. Not saying that those goals are impossible with a family, but the priorities in my life changed, which then meant some adapting to my life goals had to be done for everything to line up and start to fit together. Initially, I felt adapting meant I had failed. The fact I knew something had to give and something had to be changed, in the end, made me and my family happier, which I would call a win. So yes, adapting is going to happen; it may be less severe, or it may be an entire overhaul like I had to do six years into my career that I believe was headed full speed at an exponential climb towards greatness. What I defined as "greatness" also had to adapt. I now see greatness in the growth and development of the smartest 2-year-old (Yes, I am biased). I see greatness in seeing my spouse for more than 6 months out of the year. Bottom line, know it is ok to adapt and it is completely normal to adapt. However, be wary of changing your goals too often. This should not be a weekly event. Allow yourself to finish goals instead of always moving the finish line. And finally, when you have set goals and adapted goals, follow through and crush them. When you get the chance to perform and succeed, take it, and run.

Tactical Tip #1: Build a goal sheet for your life. My personal goal sheet includes five Sections to emphasize balance: Family, Job/Finances, Health, Education, and Leisure. I start by building Life Goals, then break those down into 10-Year Goals, and further into One-Year, more executable, goals. By breaking goals up this way, it ensures my One-Year goals are consistent and lead to the achieving my long-term goals. When setting goals for yourself, continue to analyze them and revisit them over time. Adapt where needed and tweak them as your path/career changes over time. Change is ok, but make sure you develop smart and measurable goals along the way.

<u>*Life Goal Examples:*</u>
Family Life Goals
-Forever Marriage
-Good Relationship w/Children
-Good Relationship w/ Parents/Siblings

Education Life Goals:
-Continually Learn/Grow

Job/Finances Life Goals:
-Retire as an Executive
-Retire at 62
-Maintain $15K/monthly Cash Flow

Health Life Goals:
-Live a Healthy Lifestyle
-Smaller than 34" Waist
-Run a Race at 70

Leisure Life Goals:
-Have a detached wood workshop

<u>*10-Year Goal Examples*</u>
Family 10-Year Goals:
-Have 2 Children
-Annual Family Vacation

Education 10-Year Goals:
-Get 2nd Master's Degree

Job/Finance 10-Year Goals:
-Annual Income > $250K
-Retirement Accounts > $500K

Health 10-Year Goals:
-Run a Race in All 50 States

Leisure 10-Year Goals:
-Have a Mobile Workshop
-Take 5 Woodworking Classes

<u>*One Year Goal Examples*</u>
Family One-Year Goals:
- Special Event with Spouse Monthly
-Create Joint Vision+Goals with Spouse
-Find an Affordable Vacation Location

Education One-Year Goals:
-Apply to Master's Classes

Job/Finance One-Year Goals:
-Ask for Promotion
-Make $5K from Other Than Salary Work
-Invest $18K, $1.5K/month

Health One-Year Goals:
-Weekly Push-ups and Sit-ups
-Monthly Timed 1.5 Mile Run
-Run a Race in Six Different States

Leisure One-Year Goals:
-Take a Woodworking Class

Success In All Phases of Life

Perhaps this is jumping on a moral soapbox, but the perk of being the author of a book on success is being able to define what long-term success means. The truth is that it depends; however, the same actions that make you successful in the workplace can be applied to literally every aspect of life. Balance is an integral part of my definition of success. If you have spent your life building a fantastic career and, on your deathbed you are alone, I dare say you missed the point of life. I want you to succeed in all parts of your life, you will see that most of our examples are work-related, but think about how they can apply to your significant other, your family, or your supporters. Will that work task that you "had" to complete instead of keeping plans with your family or friends make a difference five years from now? Probably not.

In a Department of Defense leadership course, the instructors taught the class that everyone has their own "utmost." In other words, everyone has their own breaking point or even ceiling of success for that particular day. I learned this lesson on a five-story repelling wall in Fort Benning, Georgia. The same wall where Army Airborne trainees have trained for decades. I do not have a particular fear of heights and the engineer in me trusts the harnesses, ropes, and training provided by the instructor will keep me safe. I was able to step to the edge of that rappelling wall, turn around, lean my body over the edge until I was parallel with the Earth, and in four leaps land safely on both feet. That was not difficult for me. However, for a classmate, that five-story wall represented overcoming a deeply rooted fear. She was terrified of heights, and before she even approached the edge of the tower, she was paralyzed with fear. After minutes of pep-talking from the jumpmasters and teammates, she retreated down those 117 steps back to the ground floor. Nearly an hour later, and with lots of encouragement from another classmate who escorted her back up the tower, she finally rappelled down that wall. Her breaking point was different from mine. Physical challenges, such as climbing down a wall, usually present easy to see breaking points, but remember that breaking points come in many shapes and sizes. It could be aging parents, problems with a spouse, a challenging project, or several other events. How does the idea of utmost and success in all phases of life relate? Just as everyone has their own utmost, everyone will have their own definition of success for each aspect of their life. If being a CEO does not excite you, then it is perfectly fine to not have it as a goal of yours. You must realize that others around you are in different phases of life and may have a different vision of the future than you do. A balanced view of success, one that goes beyond your goals in the office, will ensure you are keeping a holistic view of your life. Again, the tips provided in this book extend beyond the office and can benefit your goals in other parts of your life. I challenge you to extrapolate the work-related examples and apply them elsewhere.

Ownership of Your Job

Being Transparent

Another overarching theme for success is taking ownership. More times than not, people are afraid to admit they are wrong or that there is a problem. There are many reasons for this reaction. It could be because the person may realize they did not do something to prevent the issue or do not understand the problem enough to clearly understand what is going on. The fear of confrontation leads to either sugarcoating information to make the issue look better or avoiding the situation altogether. In fact, being transparent and owning up to mistakes can be incredibly valuable within the workplace. Being transparent forces humility, as you have to fess up to your mistakes. It breeds trust, as you admit to your coworkers and bosses when things are not going well. Companies that are not transparent, and that lack trust, suffer from symptoms of those flaws, like higher rates of turnover. You may think that the company you work for right now is not transparent; however, that culture change can start with you, or said another way, the culture change will not occur if you are not transparent.

I once went to a seminar called the Landmark Forum, a global professional development program, and although I could not relate to everything they taught, they discussed how being open about a failure or problem does not make people think less of you. People respect you more because they know you are more open and trusting, and at the end of the day, you are just as human as they are.

When you take ownership, there becomes an entirely different level of pride in one's career, project, and overall life. When your name is assigned to something, you tend to take the task more seriously and care at a whole new level. Think of it like renting a car and how you treat a rental car versus a car you own. Yes, I hope we all treat rental cars well, but the fact of the matter is that because it is not yours, that connection and ownership is typically not there.

In the classic Disney movie, "The Lion King" there is a scene where the king lion, Mufasa, takes his son, Simba, the prince, to an overlook and says, "Everything the light touches is our kingdom." Mufasa's quote sums up how I feel about ownership and is dead on how I handle a unit or group I am responsible for. Anything that my group's name is assigned to or anything that one of my people is involved in, I too am a part of, and at the very least will take responsibility if something goes south. I want people to know that I have their back and am accepting ownership of the good, the bad, the ugly, whatever that light touches is ours as a team, and I will do whatever is in my power to protect it all.

I subscribe to the principles laid out in "Extreme Ownership," by former Navy SEALs Jocko Willink and Leif Babin. Even if I did not physically provide an action to invoke a negative result, if it is in my span of control or influence, I take ownership of it. In all reality, this means that I end up taking ownership of a lot that I may only be tangentially involved in.

When NOT to Take Ownership
At what point do you not take ownership and walk away or say no? Ownership can be great, but you also want to be cautious with what you commit to and put your name to. As you will find later in the book, this can tie very close with building your brand. Putting your name to something and ownership overlap in many areas.

I am not telling you to run and cut ties any time something goes wrong, in fact, that is the opposite of what I would recommend. What you should not take ownership of is a situation or issue that seems unethical and does not sit right with your moral compass. In cases such as these, you should adamantly not take ownership.

When to give the ownership to someone else is also beneficial to know. Allowing someone else to receive praise for a "win" can do a lot for an unsung hero who deserves it. They may be that person who will never take the credit they deserve. Be a good teammate and push them out in front, let them receive the recognition they deserve. This may instill more confidence in them and create a new level of productivity in that individual. This ties into creating an environment where ownership is promoted and expected.

Creating an Environment of Ownership
Once you have developed the habit of accepting ownership, the next thing you should focus on is establishing that environment around you, where taking ownership in all things is the norm; something commonly practiced every single day. Everyone around you should want to find that connection, that level of pride in everything they touch and put their name to. Sadly, without a shining example, one that shows why ownership matters and provides benefit, many within an organization will be hesitant to take ownership themselves.

Taking ownership is extremely important in the job you perform and the environment around you. Without it, it can be difficult finding a level of identity that is needed to succeed and see results at work. Ownership is shared too; it is not just something on an individual level. Grow yourself to take ownership, strive to develop it, and then work to build those around you to do the same thing. Create that environment where ownership is a good thing. What does an organization that takes ownership of its work look like?

I recall sitting at in an aircraft maintenance production meeting, a meeting in which each maintenance squadron provided the status of aircraft and equipment for the day. These production meetings were an opportunity for management to see if maintenance actions are on time and when an aircraft will be ready to fly. It was like a typical conference meeting with the boss at the head of the table, middle management at the table, and then some support folks and subject matter experts sitting along the walls on the outskirts of the room. In the Air Force, these meetings are notorious for being brutal, emotional events. If the boss discovered that the previous day's best-laid plans fell short and there were setbacks, delays, and mistakes uncovered, someone usually got chewed out. By the time of this particular morning, I was well established in my position and my bosses trusted me. I also had a relatively long time with my immediate subordinates and we were performing well, firing on all cylinders. For whatever reason, my subordinate made some poor calls the night before, and we were severely behind schedule due to some easily prevented mistakes. As per usual, the night shift subordinate came along to the meeting with me. As I briefed my boss, I could see his frustration start to boil over. He asked what happened and I told him that I had not provided explicit instruction to my team before leaving the previous evening. I told him that these mistakes were mine. Just as I said those words, my subordinate, from the back row, stood up and admitted to the boss that he could not let me take responsibility for his egregious errors. The boss, surprised that my subordinate was willing to take the heat, was practically stunned. After a brief pause, he looked at the subordinate and simply said, "Do better." His frustration dissipated, and he allowed me to finish my report. After the meeting, he pulled me aside and complimented me on building a cohesive team that takes ownership of all actions, both positive and negative. My team knew I would take the heat for them; they had seen me do it on many previous occasions and had seen both me and the team grow because of that ownership.

Trust

Another overarching theme for success is trust. Trust has already been mentioned in "Ownership Of Your Job," and it will be highlighted in many other areas. Having the ability to inherently trust your bosses, peers, and subordinates will be critical to your success. The hope is that you also earn the trust of those same groups. Examining surveys from several industries, one interesting finding is that upper management is typically trusted less than upper management's own view of how trustworthy they see themselves. The same studies say that trust levels are much higher among the respondent's coworkers or immediate supervisor. The takeaway here is that those in the workplace, especially ones that do not interact with you regularly, likely trust you less than you believe you should be trusted. On the flip side, you may underestimate how trustworthy coworkers, bosses, and subordinates can be, particularly when you are new to a work center. Depending on the person and culture, they may not trust you right away, or you may not trust them. That is normal; trust can rarely be earned all at once.

There is a multitude of books that focus on trust, Stephen Covey's "*Speed of Trust*" and speaking series immediately comes to mind. Its importance cannot be overemphasized. An organization or team that does not trust is one that has to double check work, intent, and interests constantly. It is also an organization that is likely to breed a negative culture. In contrast, a high-trust organization can delegate tasks efficiently and significantly increase the amount of throughput it can achieve. You want to ensure you are adding to the high-trust culture.

A good example of a high-trust organization was seen on my last deployment. I believe everything rises and falls on leadership and this case was no different. From day one at our deployed location, we were told by our commanders that as long as our decisions were morally sound and justifiable, they would have our backs and go to bat for us. The sense of comfort we had, knowing our leadership was providing top cover, allowed us to operate effectively and efficiently during our time in country. If we needed additional supplies or had an innovative idea to change the way we did things, our leadership would hear us out and support us in any way they could. They knew that we trusted them to make smart decisions at their level and, in turn, they trusted us to make smart decisions at our level.

Getting Past "No"

One of your jobs as a leader is to facilitate forward progress within your realm of influence. You will find that most people will use a tried and true method to approach a task, and a significant amount of energy is required to change that person's way of thinking. Much like a stream of water or electricity, most people opt to take the path of least resistance. How does that translate to the workplace? Your fellow employees and peers will be naturally inclined to take the easy path and stop progressing on something at the first sign of "hard." I have found this to be accurate throughout my professional life; that is not to say I am not guilty of it myself, because I have been. But what I have learned is that to get the most out of your personnel, you have to be on the lookout for that natural inclination to suffice by taking the easiest route. Whenever you hear that something cannot be achieved, you should be ready to dig into a line of questioning to get at the root cause of the issue. Usually, you will discover that if you dig enough, you will uncover that the resistance can be removed with a little motivation and a little effort to help push through the obstacles being observed. Challenge those around you, not just your subordinates, on what they are doing by tactfully asking why or why not?

The overall message here is that you need to challenge those around you, even your best ones. The hope is that those around you will understand you will not accept a simple "we cannot do this" or "it cannot be done." You will find that as you increase influence in your workplace by consistently challenging the status quo, subordinates and peers will get accustomed to bringing you a deeper understanding of issues. Eventually, you will see both subordinates and peers asking, "Why can't we do this?" and, "How can we do this?" at their levels. They will break down those barriers and not stop at the first and easy "no."

Tactical Tip #2: Find a way to yes. Don't stop at the first "no." If you feel something sounds right, is feasible and legal, find a way to "yes." Do not accept: "No, we can't do that." or "There is no interest" or "That is not going to work," etc. Dig into the naysayer's excuses and find ways to combat them. An easy way to break through excuses is by asking "why?" or when you hear, "We can't do that" instead ask, "How can we do that?". Asking why or how might be all it takes to make breakthroughs on new approaches to solutions.

The most powerful leadership tool you have is your own personal example.
- John Wooden

Leading Self

I once had a boss that would tell me success was based on luck and timing. I am not sure I ever totally agreed with him, but success in your career certainly has aspects that are out of your control. The lessons in Leading Self are all about being prepared for the moment when opportunity strikes, therefore, creating your own luck.

Taking Advantage of Development Opportunities

Depending on your profession, your influence can be limited without the proper certification or degree. For that reason, I believe that working towards the expected level of educational experience is essential. The common saying that "you can never lose an education" is certainly true when it comes to continuing education in the workplace. There are several ways of achieving this, one way is by taking advantage of trainings that are offered and paid for by your employer. It is a bit of a balancing act, as you want to get as much training as you can, without giving off the perception that you are always in training, and avoiding "real work." Many companies will fund your certification, or trip to a conference, if it is relevant to your job. In my experience, I have seen training opportunities go unused because: 1) they are not sought after by the employees; 2) employees do not know what training is available; 3) employees do not think it is worth the time and effort; and 4) bosses may be uncomfortable allowing employees to attend trainings due to the workload at the office. Whether or not you continue your education usually boils down to you being your own advocate and providing rationale as to why you want and need to pursue further education or training.

If your company does not pay for continuing education, paying for classes out of your own pocket is still an investment worth making and one that can be quickly recouped in benefit. Opportunities are also often missed because many do not see the immediate value of an investment and write it off as wasted time. Bottom line: Investing in yourself is an easy opportunity to expand your job knowledge and increase your professional network with classmates and co-workers in and out of your field.

Deciphering which courses are more beneficial than others can be challenging, but there are some characteristics when looking at courses that tend to maximize return:

1. Experiential Learning. Essentially, Experiential Learning is learning by doing, trying it out, and reflecting on it. Think about how much easier it is to learn a game of cards by actually playing the game versus it just being explained to you. The lessons that you experience tend to stick with you more than those gained through reading.

2. Separation from daily work. If you can take a class that eliminates the distraction of work, it will allow you to focus on the lessons and not about the office crisis du jour.

3. Outside Perspectives. Thinking outside of the box and getting fresh outlooks is a good thing. The book Medici Effect, by Frans Johansson, discusses "The Intersection" where people of different backgrounds come together to solve a problem, for example, a physicist and microbiologist. Bringing different backgrounds together can lead to innovative solutions. Finding a class where you are surrounded by a diverse group can help you bring new ideas to your current projects.

4. Action. A class that prompts you to act on its lessons before it is over. (Just like what is at the end of this book!) During the Landmark Forum seminar, participants are challenged to participate in events outside of their comfort zone during presentation breaks. During these breaks, I saw people make an emotional decision to call family members they had not spoken with in years. It had a profound effect on their lives and the lives of those they reached out to. That action can be long-lasting and is well worth the price of

admission. Think about how you can apply these lessons or characteristics to your life and career today.

If you aim to attend a course that will aid in increasing productivity within the office, encouraging as many co-workers as possible to attend at the same time will be exceedingly beneficial. This collective learning experience allows for faster cultural change throughout the office making it easier to implement change. One way to spearhead this is to be on the lookout for training that will improve the whole office and then advocate for the trainers to come to your location to conduct the course. This typically saves the office money and allows more co-workers to attend.

> **Tactical Tip #3**: Find a course that will send the training staff to your office location. This can make it a cheaper option for the office and can allow more of your coworkers to attend.

If you work for a mature company, they likely have a professional development program for employees. Take advantage of the courses they provide and ensure you provide feedback on how well they are being executed and how to make them more beneficial. Earlier, I mentioned that many classes could be worth the cost of admission. That is even better if that cost is on the company and not out of your pocket and, if the company is paying for the course, your management should be okay with the time and effort dedicated to the class. When you are attending these classes, be all in and fully dedicated. Let go of what is happening back at the office to maximize what you get out of the course. You want to get outside of your comfort zone with the material, grow your network, and learn something new. Always remember, learning never stops.

Tactical Tip #4: Ask a senior co-worker or your HR department about professional development opportunities provided by your company. If none are available, ask if the company will reimburse you for training offered outside of the company. Search for classes that are in line with your profession, possibly provided by the professional organization of your profession. If none, Google search for professional development classes in your area. Another good time to ask about professional development opportunities is during your initial interview and during feedback sessions with your boss or supervisor.

Being a Bro/Bro-ette

Being a bro/bro-ette…A simple statement for a complex art. "Being a bro/bro-ette," in its basic meaning, is going the extra step for those around you – not sucking up or putting on a show in front of your superiors but being genuine and helping out those around you.

This comes with time, especially in the more technical professions. You cannot help fill someone else's glass of knowledge when your glass is empty. You must study, practice, get feedback, fail, learn, and apply what you have learned. Then, when the time comes to impact someone's training or knowledge on a subject, you will be ready to pour into their "glass of knowledge" and make a positive impact. You would be surprised by how much you can share with the office to make everyone better. Just by sharing small pieces of knowledge that you learn throughout the day you can make a difference. From best practices you learned along the way to what mistakes you made and will never make again and the information you were given to succeed, all these things can and should be shared with your team. Put best by Robert Heinlein, "When one teaches, two learn."

With non-technical matters, "being a bro/bro-ette" has a simple definition. It means squashing the saying, "not my problem" and taking ownership of your environment. Its actions are as easy as picking up your workplace and common area before work, after work, and leaving it a better place than you found it. Taking the trash out instead of walking by it or helping carry stuff inside for a coworker on a hot day instead of pretending not to see them, all involve doing the right thing. Not letting gripes and complaints fester between coworkers and stepping in to assist in resolving the situation. Volunteering to do the jobs that no one wants to do and then mastering them! The bottom line, never walk past a problem, this is being a bro/bro-ette – the ultimate team player.

Building Winning Teams

Success in business is rarely the doing of a single person. Think of the all-time best sports dynasties. Yes, they typically have a stand-out performer (like Tom Brady or Michael Jordan), but the dynasties always find ways to bring out the best in their supporting players. It is similar in business, sure you can win some games on your own, but those who continually do well are surrounded by, and facilitate, successful teams. Facilitating or creating a strong team is usually difficult and involves helping your coworkers become the best versions of themselves. This means raising the level of your competition.

Improving those around you starts by first recognizing that you must put in a little extra work to improve those around you by being a good teammate. The U.S. Government puts a lot of effort and resources into training its prospective military members. There are technical schools, training events, and countless professional military classes at every stage of a career, from recruit to General. These trainings are typically accomplished/attended by military members in the same point in their career, and they provide an opportunity to compete with one another for Top Graduate honors similar to Valedictorian, or Summa Cum Laude. Those who typically get these honors not only do well with coursework but also ensure that the rest of their classmates are doing as well as they can, too – using their unrealized potential.

How do you unlock that potential, be a good teammate, and slowly build that winning team? It starts with *you*. Being a reliable person around the office, sharing the latest tech trends, helping others close deals, putting in extra time even if you are not going to get the reward, etc. This requires you to be humble. You will be helping others succeed, and you need to be comfortable with your standing in the company. A good supervisor will recognize that it is you facilitating success, which is precisely what leaders within a company are expected to do. The more practice you get as a young professional creating successful teams, the sooner you will be moved on to lead bigger and better things.

Caring for People
The simplest gesture can make a world of difference, but you must be genuine and play this off of your personality. If you try to fake that you care, people will see straight through you. If you genuinely care for people, no matter what they do, who they work for, or what background they come from, it will show. Everyone hurts; it is universal. Maybe you are not "a hugger" or do not like being "soft and emotional," but sometimes that is going to be what your peers and subordinates need. You should find an approach that is both authentic and meets the needs of those around; people are not a one size fits all, and this is where knowing your people pays off. People, at times, may require encouragement and support. Sometimes, people around you will also need you to be there to kick their butt and keep them on track. Putting aside emotions and getting (or giving) the objective perspective is other times exactly what we need.

One of the best practices I have used over the years is the age-old saying, "walk a mile in their shoes." Often, we get wrapped up in our own lives and our own desires. Having empathy with your teammates can quickly enhance the trust among the team leading to a better performance, and therefore, a more successful organization.

Caring for someone has many different forms. In some instances, holding teammates to your standard may require you to be harsher than you are accustomed. Particularly in physical or life-threatening fields, this is absolutely necessary. As an extreme example, if a firefighter is too timid to run into a burning building and the fire chief comes over and hugs him and tells him he did a great job, people in the building are going to die. In this case, the fire chief reinforced dangerous behavior, potentially harming both the other firefighters and the innocent lives in the building. The fire chief failed to be caring and instead of holding the standard, they chose to take the "easy" route to avoid conflict. Instead, the fire chief could have cared for the fireman by pushing the firefighter when he or she needed it and gave them more repetitions in a high-stress environment. Point being, the environment and situation will determine the necessary tactic to be applied. There will be times when a softer, emotional side will be needed and like mentioned before, there will be times you need to use the "tough love" side.

The Middle
In any group of people, you can usually identify your performers in thirds: top, middle, and bottom. On most teams, or in the office, you have top performers who stand out and are self-starters, they impress you, blowing your standards out of the water day in and day out. You also have those bottom dwellers who take up 90% of your time, and you see their name often, not for good reasons. But what about that middle group? The average Janes and Joes who show up and get the job done. It is usually simple to identify and praise the front runners. But if the middle group feels like they do not matter and are not even noticed, you risk demotivating them which can drive them into the bottom group of performers. How do you help them rise to the top and avoid them plummeting into that bottom gang?

1. Identify who they are, let them know where they stand
2. Empower them, give them responsibilities
3. Give them feedback and hold them accountable
4. Show them that they matter and make an effort to invest time in them

We should always be growing our replacements. If those front runners move or change jobs, who do you have to replace them? In reality, everyone in the workplace is replaceable, even though some people do not think they are. Do not have single points of failure (a position where only one person can complete a task); have alternates and backups trained so they can fill the void if a capability gap ever occurs. Giving someone in the middle group the chance to shine may be all they need to develop into a front runner themselves. Some people just need one person to believe in them and, overnight, a go-getter is unleashed.

Teaching office members "how to fish" is exponentially better in the long run than "giving them the fish." However, the investment in teaching someone a new skill or process is lengthy and not without frustrations. Keep in mind, at the end of the day, you are trying to be a force multiplier, someone who is not only a high performer, but someone who elevates the performance of those around you – this is exactly what it means to grow your replacements. Making sure your team is prepared to take over duties of another member if needed is vital to building a winning team.

For example, being someone who is pretty quick and efficient at navigating Microsoft Office products (PowerPoint, Excel, Word, etc.), it is one of the most painful things in the office to watch someone else publicly edit a document who might not have the same level of skills you do. If you jump in right away and take over at the first sign of frustration, all you create is a feeling of incompetence for the not-so-savvy editor. Instead, teach them "how to fish." Teach them some useful functions and let them play around with the program. It will show them that you are okay with them failing (learning), and if you teach them along the way, they will continue to get more proficient and grow. Then, a few weeks later, you will no longer have to help them with the program and in turn you have freed up your time by instilling confidence with your co-worker.

> **Tactical Tip #5**: The Art of Shadowing – When you know you will be out of the office or moving to a different job soon, ensure whoever is going to replace you shadows you for a few days/weeks to really get the full perspective of what you do daily. There are so many little things we do throughout the day that we do not even think about; having someone shadow you through a few days of full processes and operations will let them see everything and give them the opportunity to ask questions when they have them.

Part of building a team is also growing trust in your organization; ensuring that you have trained those around you and educated them enough to keep the ball moving forward. This will make life easier if you ever need to leave the office or hand off a project. If you fail to do this, it will make life challenging – not only will you struggle with letting go of work, but it has the potential to consume you to a level that is unhealthy. Learning to trust those around you shows that they matter, and it will breed an environment of innovation, fueled by failure, patience, and improvements. Your teammates will then be more willing to bring forward their ideas and take point when you are not around. If you retain all the knowledge, skill, and decision authority, then others will never get to think for themselves or win or fail for themselves. Empower those around you to take charge and lead. It will keep you sane and healthy during times of relaxation away from the office.

Work-Life Harmony

Like I mentioned in the introduction, my definition of success is centered around family and friends. If I am lying on my deathbed with millions in the bank but have a family that does not care about me, I have not succeeded at all. In fact, I have probably made a terrible mistake. The balance between work and everything else is hugely important, but perhaps *balance* is not the right term for what I mean. After all, there are likely to be substantial imbalances throughout different phases of life. I believe the better term is work-life *harmony*. For me, the first step in that is finding a person that understands your passions and goals, whether that person is a life partner, friend, family member, or another part of your social support system. This is not an average friend but preferably someone who more than understands your life; they want to be a part of your goals and help you achieve those goals. Finding the right support team is arguably the most critical step to success and harmony as well as a happy, fulfilling life. If your support team includes a life-partner or spouse, making time and making the most of that time is critical. On date night, do things your partner enjoys. Instead of cutting date night short to finish work, stay up an hour longer. I have broken down this harmony into two different sections: first, defining when each partner is being the "lead" or the supported, and second, the Three C's that help you keep harmony intact.

<u>Supported vs. the Supporter</u>
Today, more than ever, both spouses are working. Typically, in this situation, there is one spouse (the supported) whose career drives many of the decisions of the other spouse's (the supporter) career. There is a significant difference between being the supported or the supporter, but the fact that they are different does not make one or the other more superior. Being the nucleus or the supported also comes with a lot of pressure. Keep in mind, the fact that you are the supported does not mean that you can make decisions

alone without considering the supporter's opinions. You must also weigh the second and third-order effects that come with the decisions you make and the possible impact they may have on the other person.

Another point to lay out between the supported and supporter are each side's values along with what similarities and differences exist. Knowing what the other half values and what indeed is important to them is vital in the success of the partnership. This will aid in helping the supported make decision as well, especially when it comes down to impacting the supporter. The more you know about those around you, and not just on the surface but understand at a deeper level, will help make the relationship that much stronger and prosperous.

A lot of times in our work and life, our spouse/family/partner are our main supporters. Now, remember, your spouse decided to be part of the life you are living, just like you chose to be in their life as an equal supporter. Your lives may have adapted and evolved; you may have found yourself in a different career than you were intending. Life changes and that is okay. You should understand that both of you may not have initially signed up for the life you are living, but you signed up for a partnership and a long adventure of unknowns. With that comes frustrations, uncertainty, and stressful nights, but a whole lot of amazingness too. And in the end, maybe your spouse was only on board because they knew it made you happy, and that was *their* sacrifice. Once you have kids, the harmony becomes even more challenging. Kids did not ask to be invited to the party, you brought them. But being a part of their life and their development is your legacy and will be what you make it. Instead of missing a dance recital or baseball game, go into the office early so you can get out early and make the event.

A key for the right level of work-life harmony and growing those strong relationships at home comes down to communication. The more you and your partner at home communicate, the more smoothly plans and life tend to work out. A lot of times, the friction points in our "at-home" relationships live around two things, time and predictability. They want to know what you will be doing so that they can plan their own stuff. No one wants to sit around living through one person's life and changes, being reactionary all the time, and never knowing what is to come next. If a meeting is going to go long or something comes up, let your partner know. We have hundreds of types of communication these days, heck we have watches you can talk to and they will do the leg work. I mention expectations a lot throughout the book and this is no exception: discuss expectations and let each other know what they are expected to do or what they can expect you to do. Give them a heads up that you will not make it home for dinner or that you will need to change a plan but maybe then later in the week take them out to their favorite spot, bring take-out food home, or tell the boss you are taking a half-day and get home early just to spend extra time there.

Tactical Tip #6: Discuss the next day's schedule with your partner the night before and make sure you both are tracking the same hot items that you/the other need to attend. It may bring to light some conflicts of interest that you now have been able to work out before they blow up tomorrow 15 minutes before the event.

Work and life are an ongoing puzzle that some master and some do not. Some people get extremely good at it and have all their pieces in order, while others are struggling just to keep the pieces in the game. It is a challenge, especially when in a relationship of two high performers. There is this constant give and take. Both members can have impressive trajectories that are "going places," and eventually one may plateau. One way or another, to make the relationship work, compromises must happen. The sunshine and rainbows of life with two perfect careers, a well-rounded family, no drama, no baggage is simply near impossible. A happy, successful relationship that has ups and downs, however, is more realistic and attainable.

You must have a plan. If you are just willy-nilly planning this life, going wherever the wind blows, getting married, having kids, making moves, with no issues, then good on you. But for the other 99.9% of people, you have to have a plan. Make those 5-, 10-, 15-year goals and include your partner and family. Get on the same page. Lay it all out and be realistic. Do not hide dreams or plans you may want to attempt. Most people do not like surprises. Getting it out there now makes it less of a surprise in the long run.

An excellent way to scope it with your spouse or even potential spouse is for you both to lay out those short- and long-term plans, write them out. Do they run parallel? Or do they tend to veer off in opposite directions? If you answered the latter, then you probably need to sit down and discuss some ideas or ways where you can compromise and bring those major divergent points back towards a more common parallel path. Keep the compromises and sacrifices in balance, do not let it be one side always giving up something they want or believe in. Ensuring both parties get "wins" will make the other feel valued and confident, which are essential to the success of the partnership. It also makes them feel part of the team, that they do matter, and the supported member is taking them into account.

Be resilient. If you are not expecting to fail or have hard times, well, you are already setting yourself up for failure. Life is not always 100% correct or on point, and well, there is no secret equation on how to make the perfect harmony between work and life. Going into it knowing that there will be trials and hard times is a good start, walk yourself through scenarios of failure or if something does not quite go as planned. How would you react? Let's say you and your spouse were expecting to be moved to the west coast by year three, or you want to have your first child by year five. What gets in the way? Maybe it is taking a bit longer at work to get into the job, or a long-term geo-placement in your job has presented itself, perhaps you will be gone for 6 to 18 months. Or maybe there is a family emergency going on that sets you back, or you are required to go back to school or procure extra training for a job move. Things like this are going to be out of your control and will present themselves. Being prepared and walking through different courses of action will help you not be blindsided and will give you an idea of how to handle it. You will be handed many challenges along the way, especially in trying to find a harmony between work and life. The challenge is not going to define you or where you are destined to end up, but "how" you handle that challenge and show resiliency through it, that is what will set you apart.

In life, you have family, friends, and co-workers all around you. Recognize that you are not in it alone and admit when you need help and support. There are people around you who are there to help you make informed decisions and be resilient through tough times. Do not suffer in silence. People have a hard time admitting defeat or asking for assistance, set pride aside, and know when you have hit your limit.

Be ready to work. All good things come with work. Like anything, if you think it is just going to land in your lap and be a cakewalk, think again. You will grow with each other, and with that comes new trials and new sides of one another you have never seen, and heck, they may be learning a little bit more about themselves along the way.

Be patient. This is a hard one. Time is critical and most likely you want fast results. When it comes to working with a partner remember it may take time to change your behaviors, or help them shift their behaviors. You are a product of experience, just as they are. Some good, some bad, some life-changing. You may or may not know their whole stories and what experiences drive their behaviors. What you owe them as partners is patience and support.

The Three C's of Work-Life Harmony
Communicate expectations: Throughout this book, you will read about setting expectations for yourself, your subordinates, and even for your boss. Work-life harmony is no different; setting expectations for your family members and those close to you outside of work is just as (if not more) important.

Have you ever gotten into a situation where you promised your significant other that you would be able to break free from work to give them an assist. Then right as you are getting up to leave the phone rings, or your boss corners you and you quickly realize that you will not be able to make good on your promise? Everyone has been there. Is that avoidable? Maybe not, but we may be able to sharpen how we communicate those everyday expectations. You could set the expectation as this "Hey, I am going to leave early to help you, but I will call as soon as I get out. I expect that I will be able to leave work at X time, but you know how the boss can be."

The flip side of this is that you also need to make good on those expectations. You need to ensure that you are holding your end of the bargain and, if things are not going as you planned, communicate with the party that is waiting on you to explain the situation and how it will affect plans. While researching for this book, I came across a supervisor in the Air Force who set the expectation of his family came first unless by exception – meaning when his family called, he answered or if he was away from his desk, he called back as soon as he returned. He set the tone for his unit and understood and even expected others to behave the same way. He was both successful at work and home.

Power of Team

Many of you probably have participated in some sort of team. It may have been a sports team, drama club, math team, etc. A team, for the most part, becomes like family. There are times during the season where you just want to kill one another or get on each other's last nerve but, at the end of the day when it comes down to competing and succeeding, you come together and have one another's backs when it comes to anyone not on your team. You also support their successes and goals being met along the way. Bottom line, you are family and support one another through thick and thin.

I like to think of my marriage as a team. It helps keep the playing field even and keeps us focused on the "us" rather than you versus me. It is hard to keep that perspective in the heat of things, and sometimes you must put yourself in check – you are not in this relationship to be against one another but rather work through things and grow together. When on a team, you would not go making all your decisions without consulting the team, you are not a coach in the relationship and should not try to have one or the other person take that role. Yes, you may be soulmates, but more importantly, you are teammates. Couples and partners that act as a team, a combined front, stand out from those relationships that act as single individuals. They are more in sync with one another, help one another, are more considerate and compassionate; they do not walk away from a problem quickly, but instead have value in the team and work through it. We were all taught to never quit on your team. You made a commitment and there is a way through – always. Have you had a relationship that did not succeed? When you think back, did you act as a team or was one party more selfish in areas and acting as a single entity? No relationship is perfect, but there can be tools that can help you get pretty dang close. Try focusing on sharing goals and developing goals together, so you can succeed as a team.

Compromise. Regardless of whether your significant other is working, it is a fair assumption to say that they likely have their own purpose and dreams. To keep both of you on track to success, you need to prevent your paths from diverging. That means at some point both of you will need to compromise. The best way to go about this compromise is to reflect on your long term goals. Hopefully those have been agreed upon by both of you and, when you reach those points where a big decision is needing to be made, you make a call on how that decision will get you closer to your long term goals. An awesome opportunity may present itself that takes you in a completely different path, but it is not consistent with your long-term goals. A big part of this compromise is that you provide as much time as possible to discuss with your partner so a decision does not feel forced or rushed. The definition of a compromise means both sides will lose, but for a mutually perceived greater gain that is worth the sacrifice. Therefore, providing enough time to ensure each party has an opportunity to feel heard and be a part of the decision is crucial.

While compromise is vital during those big decision-making points, compromising on day-to-day activities is also essential. You are likely out there hustling, trying to become a powerhouse in the office, and that takes time; there is no way around it. This means you are probably not spending the time you would like with family. One tip that Jesse Iztler, the multi-millionaire entrepreneur and majority owner of the Atlanta Hawks posed on a *BiggerPockets Podcast* is that he sets aside three hours a day where he does only what he wants to do – running, reading, or journaling. It is not three consecutive hours, just times in the day where he focuses on himself. And because he gets that three hours, anytime his wife wants to share one of her passions with him, he is okay with it because he got his time. He is in a unique position where he may not have a boss or a fixed schedule, but you can tailor his model to work with your current situation. Just like in communicating above, honoring your commitments and decisions is an important part of making this work. Create a team-like atmosphere.

Compassion: This is all about everyone else's goals. Know that your goals may be taking away from your family members goals, maybe you are putting energy into helping your family's goals, or that your family may be "all-in" on helping you achieve your goals. In all cases, it is essential to remember to have compassion about other people in your orbit. Be compassionate about what others want and support them with any excess capacity you can muster to help make their dreams a reality.

Building Your Brand

Have you ever heard the phrase, "This is definitely a 'John' product"? usually followed by a large, disappointed sigh? That is basically the antithesis of a positive personal brand. Building your personal brand shifts your mindset to think about what you are putting your name to and how your interactions may shift others' opinions of your work and personal skills. A 2015 Nielsen study showed that 59% of respondents said they would buy a new product from a brand they trusted versus one that is unknown. I would guess that more than 59% of your superiors or coworkers think about your brand before tasking you with projects. Is your brand one of mediocrity? Or is your brand inspiring, trusted, and proven? There is a lot that goes into your personal brand – it encapsulates your work ethic, the quality of work you produce, how you treat people, and even how you dress. Do you remember those PC and Mac commercials where the PC was represented by a conservative, dull, and unexciting character, and the Mac was represented by someone who was cool, smart, and bold? I would much prefer you be the Mac versus the PC, but more important than what type of brand you are, I want you to be aware that whether you like it or not you have a brand. Just like an item on the shelf in a store, you will be judged on your brand. So, what can you do about it?

> **Tactical Tip #7**: Identify your "why." Think about your job, your duty, your mission, and ask yourself, "Why? Why do we do it?" One of the best ways to motivate yourself and those around you is to pinpoint your **why** and celebrate it. When you see a victory, highlight it, and celebrate it. If it takes you or any member of your team longer than a split second to answer the question, "Why do you do it?" then you must take massive action to get everyone back on track, including yourself, or you will face failure. Defining your team's "why" early and emphasizing it often will get everyone reading from the same sheet of music right from the start. It will motivate your team in your times of need and bring everyone closer when every factor is working to rip you apart.

In marketing, a popular measure of a brand is a Q-Score. This rating comes in both a positive or negative rating, and it correlates to how a brand is liked (positive) or disliked (negative). The Q-Score is calculated by multiplying the familiarity score by the popularity score. To be useful, compare the Q-Score to other products that are similar to the product being promoted.

There are two things at play for the Q-Score, whether the brand is known and then whether it is liked or disliked. In marketing, it can be used to tell whether the brand, or person, can be marketed or not. Bottom line: A highly positive Q-Score is valuable. Taking it back to the workplace, you must factor two things when you evaluate how valuable your brand is: whether or not your brand is known, and if the general sense is liked or disliked. What happens when your brand is mislabeled?

I had a situation where one of my employees, Steve, had a negative reputation with upper management. The weird part was Steve was one of my best employees. He came from a diverse background and because of that had different experiences. Steve always looked at changing the status quo. He had a knack for innovation, a quality severely lacking within the unit. Steve was new to the unit, and his shop had several safety incidents in a short amount of time, so upper management instantly wrote him off. When I first heard upper management say that Steve was struggling and that we should consider that he be replaced, I was stunned. I quickly realized that part of it was my fault. I did not highlight his positive qualities as much as I could have. Part of it was Steve's fault; he was laser focused on optimizing his shop, and he did not care what his brand looked like to outsiders. The first thing I did was met with him one-on-one, providing honest and transparent feedback. I told him I thought highly of his work performance and his initiatives improving the shop. And then I explained that, at the moment, he did not have a good reputation with upper management and we needed to fix it. I took every opportunity to brag about Steve in front of our bosses. I drew their attention to the positive changes he was making within his group. In short work, his Q-Score (figuratively) went from negative to positive. He was eventually promoted to work directly with me leading operations within the organization. Because of the activities we initiated, he and I experienced some of the most success yet in our professional careers.

One concept that was shared with me from a senior executive at Wright Patterson Air Force Base was that you should think of yourself, your attitude, your accomplishments as your brand. Much like a company, everything you do impacts your brand. You decide if you will be the Mac of the office or if you will be the PC. When you embrace this concept, it will assist you in keeping a perspective on how you behave. The sales pitch you gave last week, did that help or hurt your brand? Will your customers or colleagues be loyal to your brand? Remember that your brand does not start or end at the office doors. I am sure most can think of a time where a coworker went wild during an after-work happy hour, whether you like it or not, that affects your brand.

Can't Control IQ, Can Control Work Ethic
One crucial part of your brand is your work ethic. Some out there are blessed with incredible talents. Some may have a high IQ, be charismatic, or be funny. You cannot control a lot of that, but one thing you can control is your work ethic. I am not saying you must work long hours to be successful but, when you are at work, be the hardest worker in the room. This is no different than world-class athletes. Athletes certainly need some God-given talent, but those are wasted if they do not out-hustle and out-prepare the other competitors.

Think of your brand as the feeling you leave people with when you walk out of the room. Does it bring a positive feel and raise the energy levels of everyone around? Or does it cause people to scatter and flee the scene?

An important part of your brand is how you communicate with others. Think about the brand the stereotypical cable company customer service experience creates. It typically makes you think of delayed response times, unclear or incorrect instructions, and plenty of frustration. For many, this leads to ending the relationship between the customer and the cable company. When your coworkers, customer, or upper management calls you, try to remember that how you communicate on that phone call is part of building your brand.

One of my mentors always said that people will not necessarily remember what you say, but they *will* remember how you made them feel. This can be applied to the office where if you are given a task or are appointed lead on a project and the project is a huge failure, you will almost certainly be remembered as the person who flopped and probably not be trusted with a large project for the foreseeable future (side note: sadly this is due to poor leadership - - if you fail, your boss should make you lead as soon as the next opportunity arises, not wait. You are supposed to jump back on the horse after you fall off, not walk home). But the same also holds true if you knock the project out of the park. You will be known for your above-average work and most likely be given more and more responsibility because the boss has a positive feeling from you. If you are the first scenario and do have that failure happen, own up to it and work to fix it and improve. Yes, people will remember the failure but the more you work to succeed and improve, that will eventually overshadow the failure. The bottom line is do not be afraid of failures or how people may perceive you– learn from them, grow, and crush what is in your control.

Create a Brand That You Want to Follow
Your brand should be valuable and relatable. If you have the time, invest some deep thought into the creation of your brand before you launch a company, start your career, or restart in a new job. If time is not on your side, however, do not delay business and getting results to perfect your brand. Brands change over time; just look at any major company that has been around for more than ten years. Get yours going, get something out there to the public that gets you excited, and then watch it develop and grow. The key point is starting.

Practice the Important Things

An essential aspect of leading yourself is to control what you can control. This could not be more true and tends to be what people do not get right when it comes to being prepared for a major career moment. This could be a critical presentation to clients, pitching an idea to a boss, or trying to land a new contract that will take your organization to the next level. Tom Brady knew that every Sunday during the fall, he would have the opportunity to lace up his cleats and had limited opportunities to show the world his skill. Or consider an actor in a play. The lead only has one shot at nailing a line. What do both the football player and actor do in preparation? Practice. It is baffling that we do not practice our profession like professional athletes or entertainers. Our workplace contribution to society is arguably more important than either the outcome of a sporting event or how well a play is performed.

Practice and repetitions are required to be successful in the workplace. According to *Talk Like TED* by Carmine Gallo, the average TED talk, which lasts roughly 18 minutes, is practiced 200 times before its given. If you practiced an 18-minute speech 200 times, you would probably be able to give it pretty well too. Next time you have a presentation to the boss, pretend you are going to be recorded and will be forever saved on YouTube. Study what you are saying like Tom Brady studies game film or Steve Jobs practiced his product presentations. You will be better for it.

One of the best illustrations of *practice* that I have heard comes from the renowned life and business specialist, Tony Robbins. He starts with the rhetorical question of "What is a task you are really good at?" He suggests to the audience the task of tying your shoes. Most people would agree that they are proficient in tying their shoes and have been for many years. The end of this exercise is simple but powerful, as he concludes by saying that the reason why you are confident and competent at tying your shoes is because you have done it every day since you were a small child. Anything you practice every day, and practice it perfectly until you cannot get it wrong, you will eventually excel at. A lot of other factors go into this, obviously. Still, the underlying and universal truth remains: Perfect practice makes perfect performance, yet even when you believe perfection has been achieved, remember there is always room for improvement and growth.

Everything was hard before it was easy. Brian Johnson runs a podcast called *Optimize*, and one morning had a session on "Practice." Brian went on to discuss how every single thing we do in life is hard at first and we only get better by practicing. Tying our shoes, writing our names, driving a vehicle, all were hard at one point and now may seem like second nature. Elite athletes were not born with the ability to run a sub-four-minute mile or perfect a winning slap shot into a hockey net, they got to that point by practice, practice, and more practice. We all want to be excellent, but it comes down to who is willing to put in the time and who is willing to practice. What will you practice today?

There are people out there that are naturally talented at one skill or another, and they do not require much practice to stay decent at that skill. But, it is challenging to be good at many skills without preparation. In order for you to be successful in the workplace, you will likely need to master several skills. That will require practice.

On my mirror, I have a note that says, "When it counts, practice." I have made it a point to practice for the big moments in my professional life which has bled into my personal life. Every speech or presentation I give has been written down several times, been practiced several more, tweaked, and practiced some more. Because of that, there have been very few times that I can reflect on an event where I had to bring my "A" game and think I missed the mark. Does that mean I have been perfect? No, absolutely not. There are dynamic situations that you simply cannot practice beforehand. But if you can practice to the point where you hit home runs every time the spotlight is on you, it will build a lot of credibility that can get you through some shortcomings in other aspects of work.

Now the hard part is committing and setting aside time to practice. Most people say they will practice and they simply do not, or do not practice as much as they should. You can either make excuses or make it happen. If you make excuses on why you cannot find time to practice, then do not expect to get better. Those who are motivated and able to work time into their schedule the important things will get results and get better.

> **Tactical Tip #8**: Find the most effective way to practice your craft. You may find the best way to remember a pitch is just by repetition, or maybe it is writing it down over and over, then repeating it over and over. I would also recommend you have someone listen and critique your work. If you will be in a situation where you will be asked questions, build a list of possible questions (better yet, ask others what they would ask you) and be prepared to respond to them.

Time Management

Time management is one of those things that should seem easy to nail down, but as it turns out, it usually is not. Time management skills can make or break you in the workplace, and in overall life, so it is critical to get it right and continually practice at instilling those good time management habits. So how do people become great time managers and is it something that happens overnight? Sadly, no, there is no quick fix as it is something that is acquired over some time and falls into a person's habit. Habits do not occur overnight, but with time a person will become better at it. On average, it takes more than two months before a new behavior becomes automatic. And how long it takes a new habit to form can vary widely depending on the behavior, the person, and the circumstances. In a 2009 study, health psychology researcher Phillippa Lally, found it took anywhere from 18 days to 254 days for people to form a new habit.

I remember that feeling as a middle schooler showing up to volleyball practice fifteen minutes late because my parents and I got out the door late. I depended on my parents for rides at this point, and well, the blame could go in any direction. Not the point currently. What happened, though, was I was publicly called out by the coach in front of the team who I had let down and, to make matters worse, the team had to do fifteen suicides (sprint runs), one for every minute I was late. I mean, public humiliation was already not a favorite past time of an awkward twelve-year-old trying to be cool, but now everyone is going to get smoked because of me not being on time. Did it happen again? Heck no. For me, this was a significant emotional event that would alter my life forever – funny as it may seem, this small, one hour of middle school volleyball practice ended up being an event that would permeate through the rest of my life and create a change where from that day forward I made every effort to be as early as possible. If I was not fifteen minutes early to events, I seriously started panicking, feeling that I was late. I am now that person who sets five alarms to ensure I wake up and never sleep through an alarm, and I give myself buffer time when driving to appointments or meetings because who knows if I get a flat tire or robbed along the way. Yes, I am probably a little more extreme when it comes to time management, but it is only because I cannot tolerate being late now. There is a lot more depth that goes into excellent time management skills and creating those habits, so let us break it down:

1. Respect. Being on time shows you respect the other people in the meeting/appointment. You value their time and put effort into being where you said you would be. It is about commitment and taking it seriously. We have all seen the upper management's face during a meeting when they see someone walk in late and disrupt the group. It also can impact a first impression or how people perceive your 'brand' as previously discussed. Control what you can control, and being on time – for the most part – is in your control. Additionally, if you are leading or organizing the meeting, start and end it on time. This goes a long way with your coworkers, and if you are continuously late and the meetings go over, or never start on time, sadly, that is what they will remember more than the content of the meeting. Respect others' time and use it wisely.

> **Tactical Tip #9**: If you are running a meeting and notice you are running out of the allotted scheduled time but find you need extra time, ask the attendees if they are ok going over and also allow people to leave if they need to.

2. A meeting you have organized is only *one* meeting. Your appointment/meeting is not the only thing going on during the day. Other people may have shifted important items to attend your meeting at the time requested. There also may be meetings backing up to the current one, so starting late can cause the next to start late, and so on. Just remember there are a hundred other items going on that you may not be fully aware of.

3. Be dependable. Be the person who people can count on to show up when you said you would. Avoid being the person who is known for always being late, those people are hard to plan around, and being late can cause a ripple effect that

has second/third-order effects that you may not see. This is also an item that has the potential to be part of your brand. Being known as someone who is on time and dependable is undoubtedly something to strive for.

4. Scheduling matters. Keep track of your work-life, personal life, and everything in between. Write it all down and keep an organized calendar with reminders. If you only need a fifteen-minute reminder, then use it, or if you are like some of us that need that 24-48 hour out reminder to ensure we are prepared, plan accordingly.

> **Tactical Tip #10**: Creating a shared calendar with people in the workplace helps keep one another accountable, and setting reminders will keep you ahead of the game. For home life, create a shared calendar with your significant other/family so that you can compile everyone's appointments/meetings in one location.

5. Communicate Change. Life happens and there are times where you cannot avoid rescheduling or being late. It is okay and more times than not, it is fixable, but only when it is communicated. Maybe you get sick, maybe a life event happens, let people know. Call ahead and tell them you are running 15-20 minutes late. Call to reschedule, if needed, and be sincere. Everyone is human, and people just want to be informed so they can adjust as needed.

Time management is a habit; people that never work at it will never be good at it. It takes practice and constant effort to ensure you are keeping up with it all. For most of the population, we handle our lives and work the best we can to keep it organized. Bottom line: Work to be on time and make it a habit, create schedules and stick to them, and communicate change.

Be Present

There is a difference between being at work doing your job and being a contributing, proactive, and productive member of the team. Being present will set you apart from other leaders and make you someone who is remembered positively. When you interact with your co-workers or subordinates and communicate, focus on being engaged and present in the conversation. Active listening is a crucial skill to practice when being present. What most people do while in a conversation is think about what they are going to say next while the other person is talking. This has the potential to come off as selfish and will almost immediately cause the person you are conversing with to write you off and not want to re-engage, particularly if it is the first conversation you are having with him or her. Just Listen! Really listen to what is going on, and try not to think about what you will respond with. Remember what they tell you, pay attention and follow up.

Do not only be mentally present but be physically present, attend all the office events you can. Make an effort to go to things your work is putting on. Do not be that guy or gal that never shows up to anything to the point you no longer get an invite. Sometimes attending these events outside of work grows relationships and breaks down some of those potential barriers, opening a whole new world of trust. Those barriers could be insecurities, different work or social group than you are familiar with, and overall just getting out of your comfort zone.

> **Tactical Tip #11**: Work on physically facing people when you are talking with them and keeping eye contact while talking. Avoid bad habits like fidgeting, looking at your feet, and checking your cell phone or computer while having a conversation.

Persistence
Another fundamental item that ties into practice, and keeping at it until you get proficient, is persistence. This goes hand in hand with practice. How bad you want something will show in how hard you go after it. If you are a "one setback and quit kind of person," then you probably are a person who will end up in your parent's basement with an average job, inheriting your mom's cats when she passes away. If giving up is in your current vocabulary book then you need to rip that page out and listen. Do you think Elon Musk, Bill Gates, Jeff Bezos, or even Kylie Jenner walked away or gave up after one failure? Nope, and now are some of the most influential members in society.

Positivity
Being positive is contagious; on the flip side, it can be exhausting being around negative people. All it may take to turn a work environment around is a little positivity and better attitudes in the workplace. The last item in "Practicing the Important Things" is being positive, and more importantly, is not being negative. Is there a difference? I would argue there is. I once worked with a guy who was a mascot of a university. He had the perfect persona for that; he was always upbeat, always had energy, he was always overly positive. I am not saying be a cheerleader out of bed every morning, but your daily baseline should be positive. When you walk in the door in the morning, you should try to put a smile on your face and start the day with a positive mental attitude before talking the challenges of the day.

Why does being positive matter? A positive workplace is one where, typically, you can hold yourself and others to high standards without knocking each other off your game. Positive workplaces usually assist in getting through hard times. For example, if you have an important presentation to give, you want your coworkers to help boost your confidence, to motivate you, to capitalize on the experience instead of saying, "Wow, that sounds like it is going to suck." Being positive and open-minded can also help facilitate innovation and new ideas.

However, beware being overly positive can create mixed signals. As a supervisor, in most cases, you do not want to be too positive when one of your subordinates misses the standards that you set. For one, they may think that you approve of a lower performance, therefore, dis-incentivizing greater performance; the other possibility is you come across obtuse. I once had a boss that tried to be supportive. They would comment on how great I, or my coworkers, did, even when I either did not contribute much or did not do well at all. It came across as disingenuous and as if he did not know what was going on.

Talking about why negativity can hurt not only your performance but those around you is easy to do and to comprehend. Negativity can destroy the energy around the office, and can spread like wildfire. Have you ever worked with someone who was cynical about everything? The person that points out why every new process, product, or idea will not work. It is exhausting, and it is hard to improve on anything. If you work in one of those environments, try to change it. Ask why they do not think it will work and have them suggest ways to find a solution. Be that positive influence in the room. Assist in keeping the work environment positive. Be positive to those people that may be getting ready to give a big presentation. Help make them feel confident and powerful as they approach the challenge.

The key take away is that if you cannot be positive all the time, that is okay, but at the very least, do not be negative.

Looking the Part

You probably learned as a child that first impressions make a difference and can be lasting, and you only have one chance to get those right. This was great advice from mom, dad, or your kindergarten teacher and still holds true as a new team member in the office. If you want to be taken seriously, you need to look like a player in the game. How you dress depends on what industry you are in and the culture of the company. I recommend before even interviewing with a potential employer, scope out how the employees dress. Are they in jeans and T-shirts, or are they sporting trendy suits? If in doubt, my advice to you is to err on the side of being professional. Even if you are wearing business casual in the workplace, make sure you are wearing clean, ironed clothes and making sure you discard items that are worn out. Unfortunately, how you present yourself will alter how you are treated earlier throughout career.

In Jocko Willink's podcast, the *Jocko Podcast*, he discussed this topic with one of his fellow Navy SEAL guests, Master Chief Jason Gardner. When Jason was newly on the team, while technically very proficient at his job, it was not until he started to more closely follow uniform and hair standards that he began to be trusted with more responsibilities and be treated as a professional. One of Jason's mentors told him that looking the part is much easier than being proficient at your job. So, if all it takes is a more professional haircut every couple of weeks in order to get more responsibility and trust, it is an investment worth making. Now, your workplace (just like mine) is likely not comparable to being on a SEAL Team. However, there is a lot to be learned from Jason's experience. Looking the part is similar to your brand. Upper management and coworkers are more likely to come to you when you look/act like a professional. More importantly, your subordinates are more likely to look up to you if you look and act like a professional.

Tactical Tip #12: If fashion is "not your thing," find an example of an outfit that "fits" your employer's culture on a clothier's website and buy the whole outfit until you become comfortable mixing and matching. Almost as important as what you are wearing, is how it fits you. You are better off buying less expensive clothes and then taking them to a tailor so they fit you properly.

Taking the First Step

Having a background in engineering, it was bound to get nerdy at some point. In a basic dynamics course, one learns that static friction, the force keeping an object from moving, is generally stronger than dynamic friction once an object is moving. I am sure you have felt this in practice many times: it is difficult to first move a heavy box across the floor but once it begins to move it becomes easier to push. Getting started is the hardest part. As I shared previously my bathroom mirror has, overtime, collected some of my favorite and most heartfelt motivational sayings. Another one of those fundamental sayings is sometimes you need to move out and take massive action on a goal in order to become motivated. Motivation does not always come first.

This section is all about taking the first step on a project. It can sometimes be the debilitating factor, and you succeed or fail on how you begin. Say you were given a project, or it was something you wanted to accomplish for a long time. However, it is a new initiative, it is not something that has been done in the recent past by any of your coworkers or maybe ever at all. It is up to you to clear through the initial ambiguity, define an end state, break the problem down into chunks, and figure out a way to get after those smaller problems. That is what taking the first step is all about. What if you have a team? Do not forget to bring them into the fold. Let them help you brainstorm how to break those tough projects into smaller, more manageable chunks or to find ways to break the static friction in order to make headway and bring you closer to your final product and goal.

Tactical Tip #13: Google or YouTube search a piece of a project that you have been putting off. You can literally learn how to do anything these days by searching for it online.

One thing you can do, not only in work but in life, is look for the next step of progress that requires minimal resources. I heard this great example from a talented real estate investor named Bryce Smith who was being interviewed by the *BiggerPockets Podcast*. He was just starting and trying to get out from under a car payment, but he had no idea how to sell his car without a title. What he did know was how to vacuum and clean his car, take pictures of his car, and post a craigslist ad for his car, all for little to no cost. He incrementally made steps to his goal, realizing that he had to make it pretty far in before it cost him any real-time, energy, or treasure. He applied this principle to his real estate investing. Trained as a teacher, he knew nothing about buying multi-family homes and had little knowledge on real estate, but he knew a realtor, and at no cost, he could be on their email distribution list for multi-family listings and could go view places when posted for sale. He knew he would not have to commit any money until he had Agreement of Sale on his desk.

He found that he could approach a big challenge incrementally, and with each increment, there would be known resources that would be expended. He knew at the beginning of an undertaking, fewer resources would be required. As he got further along into the process, gaining confidence along the way, he was more prepared to commit significant resources. Bryce, by the way, in six years, was able to secure $10K/month in passive income, not bad for a guy that was only 35 years old.

Five key items will assist you with this whole movement of taking that first step. Research, Plan, Pick Your Team, Analyze, Tweak, Change as Necessary, and Be Intentional.

Research. Ask the questions, observe, and find out what the goal is and what the intended purpose is for whatever you may be tasked with or signed up for. If you just start walking in one direction, well, at least you are walking, but what are you walking for? It is essential to know the rationale and reasoning behind what you are setting out to do. Not only will it keep you sane and focused, but it will also allow you to bring others along and explain when you are asked or in search of aide.

Plan. Your first step will be more confident if there is a plan that coincides along with it. Taking the first step with no plan or not even an idea of what you are walking into can be terrifying. Eliminate that stress by coming up with a plan and some options and potential outcomes. Walking through the "what ifs" and how you can react and prevent chaos can give you a needed sense of comfort. Also, you want to be able to be confident enough that you can also sell what you are doing as you take those steps. How do you expect to bring people alongside you with no plan? I mean sure, if you are that person that people would walk into a fire for, then you are probably golden, but if you do not yet have the reputation, providing a game plan for those people is key. Speaking of people, it is all about the team.

Pick Your Team. Taking a step is better when multiple people are there, in step, supporting one another. Get those members alongside you to go forth and conquer. Sell that plan and your vision to them, inspire them to want to be a part of that team. Pick a good mix. Pick the visionaries that come up with good ideas and the closers who can take an idea and put it into action. This is where you can reference back to "The Middle" and work on providing an opportunity/challenge for them to grow and become better. Take a chance on the shy guy or gal who has killer products but stays in the background. Find a balance, find the synergy that is needed, and conquer together.

Analyze, Tweak, Change as Necessary. It will not be perfect in the beginning and if you think it is, then your bar was set lower than it should have been. Keep improving and find that innovation that takes everything to the next level. Leverage your team for those ideas that turn ordinary into extraordinary. Make the changes along the way to create the masterpiece down the road. Nothing worthwhile was ever easy or perfect the first time. It took a lot of edits, work, and trial and error to get to its current level of excellence. Learn from those changes and move forward.

Be Intentional. Have a purpose, have a why, and spread it. Being intentional is important, and it prevents that grey area of confusion that can internally lead to destruction and pure chaos. Finding that purpose, and going for it, pays off exponentially in the long run. Plus, it gives focus and educates everyone on what they are working for and toward. Failure to have intent can lead to multiple start overs and wasted time. Having intent will breed confidence, and with confidence comes success.

No matter what the job description says,
your real job is to make the boss look good.
- Lois Wyse

Leading Up

By integrating the skill of leading up into your daily routine, you will be acting like your immediate supervisor. Now, I know what you are thinking, "I will not be getting compensated like my boss, so why would I want to act like them without the compensation?" It is a fair question to ask, and there may not be an immediate payoff. By helping your boss, you will free up some of their time so they can focus on bigger, more impactful responsibilities, again, you may be thinking, "So what?" Ultimately, you are training yourself to think like your boss, which will lead to either your promotion within the company or your ability to take over a role at another company more senior than your current position. Until that happens, this line of thinking will expand your existing knowledge, make you more successful within your current job, and prepare you for the next step.

The goal is to provide pertinent information to your boss at the right level of fidelity at the right time. At first glance, it seems a little weird to worry about why you would need to lead upward, lead your boss. After all they are the boss; they should be leading you. Unfortunately, a 2013 study from Gallup tells us that only 10% of people have the natural ability to be managers and, 82% of the time, companies put the wrong person in a manager role. With statistics like that, chances are your boss needs a little, or maybe a lot, of help. Even if you have one of the 10% of managers that are effective, leading up will still make your supervisor and your organization better. Everything works much smoother when you are on the same page and work together with the boss. Influencing your boss is an incredibly important part of your early success.

Leading up, as odd as it may feel, is a natural part of excelling in the workplace. Today's managers need the support of competent and proactive employees for them to excel. If you expertly manage the relationship with your boss, you will likely be a standout performer. There are some pitfalls here. Leading your boss must be a balancing act. You need to help them, while at the same time, ensuring you do not undermine them or make them look incompetent. If your effort is making up for incompetence, it will be noticed by upper management. Before jumping into the tactics, let's further explore why this leading up relationship matters so much.

When you are talented at leading your boss, you will increase the amount of trust they have in you. I have already talked about building trust with yourself, the trust between you and your boss is certainly equally as important to your success.

Tactical Tip #14: Whether you have an extremely competent boss or not, you can still find ways to lighten their load, build credibility, and become a trusted agent. Make the first move and start a conversation with your boss. Let him/her know that you are interested in learning more about [insert work topic(s) here]. Look for ways you can make your boss more successful and take work off their plate. It will give you a chance to shine and make your boss more comfortable delegating work to you in the future.

This section explains several tactics that work on building trust. After implementing them, your boss will know that you understand their priorities, and more importantly, are correctly aligning your effort and those of your team to meet those priorities. Your boss will also see that you can clearly communicate for, and through, them to their superiors without circumventing their authority. Mastering this skill involves staying a step ahead of your boss when it comes to knowing what they typically ask. This includes not only identifying what questions your boss may ask, but also providing information about your ongoing projects and your personnel before they ask for it. If you combine all these abilities, it will unquestionably increase your boss' trust. You can imagine that it does not take too many of these tactics before your boss trusts: 1) what you are doing, 2) how you are leading your team, and 3) how you are managing your projects. This trust, the ensuing flexibility, and the autonomy that trust lends you from management will be integral to your success.

Once you have your supervisor's trust, you can begin to better influence their actions and future plans. Most bosses, once they trust you, will start including or consulting you on some of their decisions. This allows you to get a glimpse of more strategic issues within the organization and makes you aware of supervisory matters well above your position. It comes full circle, as this new awareness improves your ability to lead your boss because you can better understand their needs and wants from a managerial perspective. This influence gives you the ability to broaden the authorities of your position and make a more significant impact within the organization.

By helping your boss, you likely will gain a close mentor and advocate that can assist throughout your career. This may not have an immediate impact on how you perform, but in the long run it is certainly beneficial. Your boss may rarely have someone that tries to make their life easier or reduce their workload, so what you will be doing for them will pay dividends in the long run. Having your boss as an advocate, or sponsor can help you make great strides within your company or provide a glowing recommendation if, or when, you choose to leave your current organization.

How to Treat Your Boss

Now, before I talk about gaining influence with your boss, knowing how to talk to, and about, your boss is important. Your boss is the head football coach of the office team. As much as you may not like the coach, trash-talking your coach will not make the team any better. It is likely to make the team worse. It is also imperative to treat your boss with respect, maybe even a little reverence. Making your boss look good goes a long way and makes the trust you are establishing grow faster and stronger. When they know that you have their back and feel comfortable leaning on you to assist them, the relationship turns into a team, and your ability to influence upstream increases.

Even if you think you are smarter than your boss, making it known to them or others will rarely work out in your favor. Showing aforementioned reverence may very well be seen as sucking up or brown-nosing, but you could also consider it as *loyalty*. Loyalty to the team should be valued in any company. Regardless of the supervision that you have, a level of respect should always be honored to your supervisor. Regardless of the talent of supervision, there is always an opportunity for you to be a leader and influencer within the office.

Ask for Expectations

One thing you should ask of your boss is a sit-down to discuss their expectations for you. You want to make sure with any new boss that you understand what they expect of you. You want to know where the bar is that they set for you. In order to Not Suck, you do not want to hit that bar; you want to clear that bar like an Olympic high jumper. Once they explain their expectations of you, you should lay out your expectations for them. These are not demands but rather an opportunity to tell them how you want to be treated as an employee. Things that I always say: give me your hard problems, give me space to work the issues, I want to be your top performer so demand that of me, provide constructive criticism on the spot (or not). Some other expectations that you may want to ask for are:

1. Information requirements, what exactly are they wanting (Who, What, When, Where, Why)

2. How do they like to receive information and communicate (email, call, face-to-face)

3. What information needs to be relayed ASAP and what can wait for a regular update

4. When should you ask permission and where do you have free reign

5. Expected attendance at non-mandatory events (i.e., out of regular work hour events)

Getting your boss' expectations is not a one-time deal. This should be a consistent touchpoint with projects and plans. I use this as an opportunity to check how close I am to meeting expectations with any projects. If the boss gives you a project without a clear vision for what the end product should be its like the boss telling you to take a car trip without an end location. You may originate your drive in New York City and start heading in the direction of Los Angeles, but your boss may have actually intended for you to end up in Florida. You want to check on expectations before you go too far down the road. I would much rather know I am headed in the wrong direction before I am through the Lincoln Tunnel than halfway through Ohio. It takes a lot less energy to make a small tweak in direction than to have to practically start over.

Tactical Tip #15: Ask your boss for an initial expectation session, regardless of how long you have been in the position. When scheduling this session, provide them a couple of days to think about what they will say and ensure you prepare for what you want to say. Imagine how the conversation is going to go and be prepared to tell them what you expect from them.

Know What Matters to Them

Many will tell you that keeping your head down and doing your job is the best way to find success. Keeping your nose to the grindstone is what you will hear. I have found that picking your head up and gaining the broader perspective will make you more successful, but make sure you are still getting the job done (See Leading In). Knowing the priorities of upper management at least one echelon above your boss can be very helpful. A useful tactic here is to look out for corporate messaging that allows you to know what is going on in the company. What is the CEO talking about at the stockholder meeting? What is Public Relations saying in their press releases? What is being pushed on social media? And most importantly, how do you and your efforts align with that messaging? The military has a whole faction of the press that follows what the military branch secretaries or high-level generals are saying and doing, and reports on it. We have used that large media following to keep a pulse on what is going on in the Air Force. Alone, this situational awareness buys you credibility because you know what is going on outside the confines of your office. More directly, understanding your upper management's goals and guiding your boss to highlight how your tasks and projects further those goals, can greatly help focus the work of the office. This attention will show upper management the value of your office, your boss, and ultimately you.

A key aspect of this being successful is communication. You may think that drawing attention to your office may be self-serving and, it may be, however, it is necessary. I had a boss once that was not the greatest but was far from the worst. His downfall was that he was a terrible communicator to leadership, which made him come across as a weak leader. After a failed inspection (the military has many inspections) he put together a corrective action plan. He built a team to execute it, but he did not properly convey to upper-level management that we failed, let alone, had a plan to fix it. Six weeks into the corrective action plan, his boss found out about the failed inspection and promptly fired my boss for loss of faith. It had little to do with the fact that we failed the inspection, but more that it was unknown to leadership that we had a plan in place being executed to fix the deficiencies. Ultimately a lack of communication was what led to his firing; he needed to relay what was going on to the boss. This goes both ways. If you are way ahead of schedule and well under budget but not telling your boss, your boss will likely not know. There is a bit of personal and office branding required to make sure leadership knows what is going on.

In parallel to learning upper management's priorities, you need to be able to learn your boss's priorities and preferences. It is difficult to short circuit the time it takes to learn personal preferences, especially if you work remotely or do not hear from your boss much. Personally, I want to know their priorities and preferences after being in a position six months. However, in one of my jobs, I had talked/seen my direct supervisor only once in the first two months I was in the job. With little facetime in front of the boss it was hard to gauge what they wanted, so, I dug for it. I let them know that I did not have a great feel for what information they needed or when they needed it. When in doubt, ask!

The goal is to provide information that your boss needs, before or preferably right as they need it. In a sales or an operations job, it can be as easy as the metrics the corporation tracks. Providing your boss with those metrics and, more importantly, your interpretation of those metrics, allows them to make better decisions, redistribute resources, or communicate to their bosses on the progress of the organization.

The best advice is to ask your boss what type of information they typically like to report on. You will know you are doing this well when they are not continually questioning you for necessary information. Once you know what your boss wants, you will be able to ask better questions at your level.

Tactical Tip #16: Use calendar reminders (see Time Management under Leading Self). If your boss asks you for an action, put a due date on your calendar when you need to get that information to them. If there is a recurring data requirement, put a recurring reminder. Using your phone calendar works, too.

Learn the Questions They Ask

The faster you can prove to upper management that you *think* like upper management, the faster you are likely to *become* upper management yourself. This section is about thinking like your boss and how to get ahead of their information demands.

A great way to keep ahead of the boss is to separate yourself from your biases and everyday thinking and put yourself in their shoes. Much like knowing their priorities, knowing how and what information he or she asks for is important. Luckily for you, most people are predictable, and with enough time and experience, you can figure out what information your boss typically asks. If every Monday your boss asks about weekend production and output, you should know to have that information ready every Monday. You can usually link the questions to their priorities. For example, as an operations manager for a satellite operations center, my most important priority was having a satellite in an operationally acceptable status to continue the mission. When a problem was brought to my attention, one of the first questions I would ask is, "What is the impact on the mission?" With time, all subordinates would provide me with a concise impact to our operational mission with any problem that arose without me asking for it. If you can learn what questions your boss cares about, you improve the speed and efficiency in which you can communicate with them.

> Tactical Tip #17: When in meetings with your boss, keep a running list of the questions they ask you and others. Write them down and look it over on occasion. You want to recognize the patterns of those questions to help guide what questions you are asking, or what information you think they will want to know.

There are times when you will have a boss that is not predictable with their questions. In that scenario, you will need to refine the expectations that you have with your boss. Let them know that for you to be successful, you need to know what specific indicators are driving their decisions. Then throughout the day, as seemingly random questions are asked, pull your boss aside after the fact and ask them to describe their train of thought with respect to the outcome or decision. It could be that there is uncertainty on the direction they want to proceed, and they are exploring many different paths. Once a final direction has been determined, their questioning should become more predictable.

Once you have a good feel for what questions your boss asks, you can start introducing those into your meetings if you are a supervisor/team lead. Asking yourself those questions throughout the day will cage what information you will need to provide the boss. Your goal is not only to get the information your boss needs but likely one level deeper to answer detailed questions they have. Above, I mentioned that as a team lead, I would ask about the operational impact on the mission of an issue. Putting myself in my subordinate's role, I would have asked or known the answer to the following information:

How did the initial issue arise?
Was this issue preventable?
If preventable, how would you fix it in the future?
What timelines do we have to recover?
What stakeholders will be concerned with this issue?
Should I recommend we reach out to those stakeholders?
What is the cost of the fix?
How will this affect the financials?

Now, this line of questioning is obviously leaning towards a negative event.

It is also important to understand what your boss is looking for when pitching an opportunity. Some questions that come to mind:

How will this improve operations?
What is the financial impact of this improvement/new line of business?
How much will it cost?
Can you produce a low-risk minimal viable product?
What resources are required to try this?

These are only possible questions to ask, you can likely search the internet to find a more comprehensive list. The idea is to be ready to either provide the right information to your boss and to be able to go just a level deeper with your questions. Focus on those second and third-level questions that your boss may dig into and what to know. Being overly prepared is never going to let you down; being underprepared will get you noticed real fast and not in a good way.

Communicate for Them

Now that you know your boss's expectations, priorities, and the information they use to communicate, you can now begin to communicate for them. Perhaps the most significant advantage of communicating for the boss is that you control, or at least heavily influence, the messages that are being sent. This is especially important if your boss is less than competent, which happens in everyone's career at some point or another. Communicating for your boss builds on all the steps mentioned in this chapter, ultimately leading to being able to speak for your boss. If you know they trust you, know their priorities, know the things they ask for, you should be able to easily craft a message that captures all the information that your boss would generally relay to their bosses.

There is a significant differentiation to make, the goal here is not to subvert your boss and go right to their boss, but rather to provide quality products for your boss to communicate to management. Now, you can do this with any mode of communication. However, email is probably the easiest to explain. One thing that I do is build emails that are "Ready to Send" to my boss (example on next page). Start by explaining what you are trying to achieve in the body of the email, then indicate that below a cut line, you have provided a draft email for them to edit and send along.

Ready to Send Email Example:
Boss,

We had an issue with the production line last night that will put us behind in our effort to hit our monthly production goals. Below the cut line, I have a draft email to send to upper management to explain what happened and our fix. Please edit as you see fit.

Sincerely,

Dan
----------------------CUT LINE----------------------
Mr. Smith,

Summary: Last night, the production line had an equipment issue that caused a halt of operations for an entire shift. We expect this will cause us to miss this month's production goals. However, we have found the root cause of the issue and working with the equipment manufacturer to permanently fix.

Details: At 8:05 PM, the WidgetMaker 3000 had a fault that caused a full halt of the production line. Dan's maintenance team diagnosed the problem to an erroneous error on a safety sensor. The team attempted to override the sensor but were not able to do so without voiding the machine warranty. We then called the manufacturer of the WidgetMaker, located in Switzerland, to troubleshoot. The manufacturer was able to give us an approved workaround around 4:00 AM and production resumed.

During manufacturer troubleshooting, the root cause was found to be a software issue. They are sending out a technician to install a software patch, and I have also talked with my peers to have the patch installed at our other production facilities with the WidgetMaker.

Please let me know if you have any questions.

Sincerely,

Dave

As you can see, this ensures the information that you, who is likely smart on the tactical details of the matter, find necessary is included in the relayed message. Your boss is likely to be impressed if you provide them with this unprompted.

If your boss prefers to communicate by phone, build a page of talking points that starts with the desired outcome, address the aspects they need to cover, or perhaps issues they need to avoid and give that to the boss before they make the call.

Tactical Tip #18: Next time your boss has information due, or you need assistance from them, cue something up for them in a Ready to Send email or talking points.

Pushing Information
One of the more critical steps about leading up is all about providing, or pushing, information to the boss. Similar to the previous topic, once you know what your boss is looking for, you want to push them information before they even ask. This keeps you ahead of the curve and likely provides you more freedom to work independently. This can limit all kinds of frustrations that a hovering boss can bring you. It is difficult for your boss to micromanage you if you are always ahead of them. After a while, your boss will just start responding to emails with "okay," "thanks," even the occasional "good work," because you answered all the questions they have or they have gained enough trust in you that they know you are in control of whatever situation you are informing them.

At this point you are acting like the boss and, hopefully, making your boss's life a little easier. You will not be perfect, but compared to most of your coworkers, you will be completely exceeding expectations. You are making your boss's life easier because you are a solid employee who is quickly becoming an influencer in the office and their go-to. Your boss will (or at least should) brag about you, increasing your reputation and personal brand within the company. You also have freed up some of your boss's energy, which they can reinvest back into the company, further building value in your team. Now you may ask, "Why would I want to make my boss's life easier? After all, they are getting paid more than me, have more responsibility, and now I am just making them look even more valuable to the company than perhaps they should be." Remember, this is about building and creating a winning team.

Highlight Projects and People to the Boss

I had a boss in an already high performing unit and, when we made improvements, he would frequently say that we are "working on the margins," meaning the bulk of the gains had already been realized and that we were just finding ways to get a few percent better. This is what I would consider the next segment. If you are already a supervisor, proactively finding ways to brag about your people is how you get just a few percent better. After all, many supervisors rarely recognize employees, as a survey from the global employee engagement company, Reward Gateway, showed 69% of employees feel demotivated by lack of recognition. When you are pushing information to your boss, make sure you tell them how great "Tom" is doing in HR, of how he and his team came through to make whatever result possible. By doing this, you are improving the brand of your subordinates, your team, and ultimately bettering your personal brand. You will start to see your boss bragging about your personnel, mostly because you have armed them with information for them to share. When talking to your boss or to their supervision, find ways to weave in that "you have the best team in the company" or "my team is exceeding goals," etc.

Beyond the people, you need to brag about your projects. I want you to remember these phrases, "We are working on the best project in the company" or "I have got the best job/team/problem to solve in the company because of X reason (hit a significant goal or came in under budget, etc." If you are like many employees, you only seek out your boss when there is a problem. You hesitate to tell them all the great things that are happening within your team. Take the opportunity to work the improvement margins; find ways to highlight what you are doing for the boss. Much like bragging about your personnel, you will start to notice your boss's boss knowing what you are up to only because you have provided talking points for your boss to share. This is an incredibly effective way to build the brand. Even if you do not think anything significant is ongoing, find those good nuggets of progress that you can drop into conversations, emails, staff meetings, etc. It will pay dividends.

Being able to successfully lead up can make all the difference in both your career success and overall happiness. It all starts with asking for initial expectations and asking for a one-on-one sit down with your boss. From there, you will be able to know their major calendar and tasker items, how to schedule, and keep them informed the way they want. You will start to build rapport with your boss and will learn how they operate, how they think, and what is important to them. Remember, one way this can be mastered is by keeping a running list of questions they ask and learning their patterns. In the end, being able to think like your boss helps make their life easier, them be more successful, and ultimately gives you the tools to operate like your boss with things such as the previously mentioned Ready to Send email or talking points. Strive to be better than the employee just doing their time, clocking out and heading home not entirely invested. Challenge yourself and be a productive employee who makes not only your boss but the team *that* much better.

Everything you want in life is a relationship away.
- Idowu Koyenikan

Leading Across

There are countless books, videos, speeches, and other material about how to motivate your subordinates, how to show them you care, or as I say, lead down. Similarly, many discuss the topic of influencing your boss, leading up, and influencing change in yourself from within, leading self. The topic often overlooked and critical to your success: How to lead your peers.

If it has not happened already, there is going to come a time in your life where you are going to be put in a position to lead a group of your coworkers or equals. Notice the choice of words, *lead* not *manage*. You always have the opportunity to be a leader, no matter what position you are in.

Leading your peers initially starts the same way every other level of leadership does – learning how to connect, build trust, or create rapport. What separates the peer level of leadership is that even though you might not be in direct competition or any competition at all, you are more or less on the same playing field playing the same game. This is especially true in the eyes of your superiors. The worst thing to do in this situation would be to write off your peers and immediately go to work making yourself shine, possibly at the expense of your peers. Remember, you are all working together to achieve a common goal.

This section will provide tips on how to get to know your peers and build strong relationships with them. Once you know your peers, you must then recognize when it is more appropriate to lead your peers versus when it may be more useful to be a great follower (while still influencing the team). This section ends by explaining why it is better to help your peers instead of stepping on them to get ahead and, even when you do this right, your peers still may not appreciate you.

Knowing Your Peers

A "professional peer group" is a broad term. In this section, I define it as someone who is near your responsibility level and who you have no formal authority over. Since the term is broad, it is worth mentioning that many in your peer group may not perform to the same caliber as you, may not have the same career aspirations, or have any of the same interests as you. Regardless of the differences, getting to know them is extremely important to your success. It is preferred to build these relationships before you need to actually call upon them for a favor. When creating these relationships, you are growing professional capital with your peers, capital in which you can leverage for assistance in getting the job done. For instance, if you have professional relationships with peers from all around the office and have worked to develop a good rapport with them, when you find yourself in a bind or need advice, you can turn to them for their expert knowledge.

There are many tactics to finding common ground I cover in this section, but the overall guidance is to stay humble and soak up your peers' stories like a sponge, particularly their "why" and their goals.

As you enter a new office or make the determination to finally get out from behind your desk, there are several phases of relationship building that you will experience. The first, likely as you are being shown around the office, is the speed dating round of getting to know your peers. For example, "Hey, this is Jill from accounting, she is in charge of x, y, and z." During this time, be friendly and take notes. If you are anything like me, you quickly forget all that you were told. That is okay. Not everyone remembers names and titles during this phase. What I like to do is compartmentalize the office based on functions, roles, or specialties. This helps for when I get settled, while I may not know the marketing person's name, I have a good idea where he/she sits. This leads into the second phase of relationship building and that usually comes after understanding how your role interacts with that of your coworkers. Go back to Jill a week or two later and figure out what x, y, and z actually mean and how they fit into the big picture.

When walking around the office trying to get to know your peers – be friendly in your approach and try to meet one or two new people a day. Introduce yourself to break down barriers. One of the best ways to get people to open up is by asking them simple questions about what they do and show genuine interest in their responses. Seek out people who have been in the organization for a long time and pick their brain on the ins and outs of the business that goes on inside the company's walls. You end up spending a significant portion of your life with your peers at work, some of the relationships you build will likely morph from professional to something more personal.

Getting to know your peers on a professional level typically starts with understanding what role they play in the organization. Once you learn what they bring to the table, you want to learn what they value and strive for at work – in other words, their "why." You want to be able to understand what motivates them to get the job done and what makes them feel successful. How do you find this? You observe and ask questions. What do they volunteer for in the office and what do they raise their hand for to lead or participate in? What are their strengths and weaknesses around the workplace, are they good with Excel and PowerPoint, or are they an all-star public speaker who hits a home run every time they deliver a proposal? As time goes on and you get to know them better, you can develop a healthy feedback relationship, meaning you are both cleared to offer any constructive criticism to the other.

Ideally, a professional relationship can deepen and develop into a personal relationship. This is beneficial down the road, when you really need something, they will have your back because they care on a personal level. Put in the time and effort to know the people, ask them about their lives, stay engaged, and know when to check in on them when things may not be so good outside of work. If they feel like you genuinely care and have their back, they too are more likely to have your back at work, and in life, when it counts. Find the hobbies and fun items they like to partake in their daily lives or what motivates them at home. Do they have kids and a spouse? Or are they super crazy about their nine-year-old black lab named Bud of whom they are constantly showing you pictures? Strive to ask your coworker about more than the weather. Give them a platform to talk and ask for their opinions or advice on a particular subject. People love when they are talked up, for example, "Hey, Karen told me you are the expert on all things Outlook, mind if I ask you a couple of questions?" Being genuine and relatable will do nothing but help grow your network and create deeper friendships with those around you. Just being present and engaged ("active listening" mentioned previously) with people goes a long way in building relationships.

Always remember that those whom you are building a work relationship with are also evaluating you and watching how your brand and competence ebb and flow. Strong team players value other strong team players, this makes for a connection that is not only valuable currently but will continue to be relevant in the future. You have to grow your reputation and show them you mean business; you too are here to succeed, and you want to do it the right way. Being a good team player, in the end, makes people want to be on your team, and others will likely be more receptive to following you and your example.

In Keith Farrazzi's book, "*Never Eat Alone*," he talks about how building relationships is like building muscle. It requires time and activity. He recommends sharing experiences to solidify relationships. As an example, going on an intense hike with a new coworker will bring you closer together faster than by just having daily work interactions.

> **Tactical Tip #19**: Ask personal questions about your coworkers, write it down and bring up some of the responses in a later conversation. Just don't be weird about it.

One of the most common phrases when meeting new people has to be, "So, what do you do?" We have all said it, and we have all have had it asked of us. What do you do? Many people believe that asking someone what they do is not a proper way to start a conversation. It could come off with a judgmental tone to it and immediately defines the person by what they do for work, nothing else. For better or worse, I do not think it matters what you ask new people you meet, but the real magic comes in how you ask them and how you address them. In other terms, your tact.

For starters, when meeting new people, do not be interrogating. It is usually easy to find common ground by asking where someone is from, what they are interested in, what hobbies they have, and so on. What is important here is being a humble, genuine person learning about your new connection. The primary key to success here is not trying to one-up them with every story they tell. Ask questions and listen. As my mom always said, "There is a reason we have two ears and one mouth."

When to Lead Your Peers

We have all been there, in a sea full of people and the teacher or boss asks for a volunteer. After they ask for a volunteer, what usually follows is a snarky, "Okay, not all at once" from the boss when no hands are raised. In a situation like that, where you are a little fish in a big pond, and you want to get noticed to start creating a name for yourself, I say, "Go for it!" If the opportunity presented sounds cool or sounds like something you would want to do, regardless if you currently have the skills to do it, go for it.

Of course, there are other situations where you can find a way to become a leader with your peers. Probably most common is when a supervisor assigns a group to complete a task. Regardless of how formal the project, it is vital to designate a point person or leader. Selecting that point person is highly situational, but here are a few things to think about when you walk into those first few meetings or phone calls for the project. You do not have to be the designated leader in order to be influential, so do not feel that you have to insist on being the leader. When appointing a lead to a project (if not designated by upper management), I typically poll the group and ask who wants to lead. As mentioned earlier, most people do not want to lead or are intimidated to do so. If no one volunteers, that is your opportunity to raise your hand. This starts to instill trust because the group recognizes that you allowed them to lead and, when no one else would, you accepted the challenge and, sometimes, the burden. If someone else steps up, allow them to. If you know your peers well enough, you can even recommend someone who may have a particular skill set or passion that is best suited for the project. This action instills trust and makes one of your peers feel incredibly valued because they understand that their work is being publicly recognized. The formation of the team in those first few meetings, as the project takes shape, is a crucial time to feel out the group dynamics. Be confident but not overbearing and be humble, but do not lose your voice.

How to Lead Your Peers

Whether you are the formal leader of a project or you are indirectly leading the group, knowing how to behave is incredibly useful. Especially with your peers, you want to stay humble, use some emotional intelligence, and do not try to subvert anyone's efforts but guide discussions when you feel it is needed. If you do not have anything useful to say, do not feel like you have to dominate every conversation. But it is important to have a voice so your peers recognize that you are there. Be agreeable to ideas that are decent and be willing to take small losses for a more valuable win.

Tactical Tip #20: When leading a meeting with peers, take extra precautions to respect their time. Build an agenda with the desired outcomes and distribute it before the start of the meeting. This shows your preparedness and provides you an opportunity to guide the discussion without necessarily out voicing your peers. Again, try not to be weird about it.

When and How to Follow

Just as important to leading a group of your peers is knowing when and how to take a backseat to another leader and be a dependable, willing follower. By giving someone else a chance at leading, you will start to build more leaders within your group. Additionally, when people are put out front and given the responsibility of being the leader, they begin to buy into the team, organization, group more so than if they were riding in the passenger seat. How do you know when and how to follow? Well, you probably guessed it, *it depends*. It depends on a few factors that I am going to cover and, with a little bit of experience, you will be able to determine the proper time to follow.

If you find yourself in a situation where you are new to a group, organization, or a business and you are not placed in a formal leadership role, then there is an opportunity to shine as a follower (and let the leadership roles come to you later). Even if you are not new to a group or you do not get picked when you raise your hand to volunteer, that is okay. You now have even more reason to be a fantastic follower and make your peer-leader look the best they can. By making your peer-leader look their best, it shows that even if you are not the lead role on the team, you still influence those around you and support them to perform at their best. People will want you on their team just because of the brand you have created for yourself. If you do the contrary as a follower and become a roadblock to productivity, you will bring the team down and be seen as someone who stifles results.

A few things come to mind when discussing followership and how to be the best follower. A strategy found to work is to frame the conversations to whoever is leading. Ask questions to sculpt the conversation, to influence the team, and to lead the group passively. What is meant by this is asking questions along the lines of, "Hey, do you want me to get this started?" or "What do you think our timeline should be to have this done by? I am thinking May 1st if it is due May 8th." or "How are we going to break up this task?" Those will give the leader a direction or a path to start going down to complete the project. Putting the ball in their court empowers them and lets them know that you are thinking ahead for them and have their best interests in mind.

Say you are not currently in an official leadership role, but you want to be. Again, this could be because you are new, the boss does not know you, the boss has favorites (and you are not one of them), or a reason entirely different that you may never know. Regardless of the reason, if you want to stop being the perfect follower, and you want to lead, then ask! Your boss may think you are happy where you are, or doing what you do, and has no idea that you are dying a little bit each day on the inside when you are not asked to take point on a project or presentation. Bluntly, but tactfully (of course), telling your boss that you want to lead and are ready for that challenge will only serve you well. Asking him or her if there is a project they need a lead on, or to think of you next time one comes up, is usually all it takes. Now, when the opportunity presents itself, do what Richard Branson preaches, "If somebody offers you an amazing opportunity but you are not sure you can do it, say yes – then learn how to do it later."

A few final comments to tie the bow on following a peer's lead, and this is advice that is easier said than done, but usually makes all the difference: when working with peers and subsequently leading or following your peers, you need to figure out when and where to put your foot down and draw the line. Yes, it is essential to follow your peer's lead and do your best in supporting him or her, but blindly following someone or something can become harmful if left unchecked. The checks and balances you create for yourself can span from drawing the line on office gossip when it gets to be more than a fun jest, to having a solid stance on office ethics and demanding those around you to follow the same rules, and especially to holding your fellow peers accountable. Giving the feedback, good or bad (good is usually way more comfortable to do, but bad is more important), will take time to get right and probably require some trial and error over awkward conversations. To ease the harshness of feedback, I recommend you sandwich constructive criticism with positives. Providing constructive feedback will only make yourself and your peers better. Bottom line, do not let standards and expectations dwindle regardless if you are leading or following your peers. Ask questions if things do not seem correct or accurate and do not fall in the trap of group-think, or going with the flow, just to avoid an awkward conversation. If something is dumb, dangerous, or different, say something; do not let it grow into something that could become physically, mentally, or emotionally harmful to those around you, including yourself.

Start peer-to-peer feedback sessions with criticism aimed at your own performance (it is likely you are not perfect) and then ask the team if there is anything else they would have improved on, if no one says anything, provide criticism by saying, I think we could have done X better...what do you think? (directed at the person who was responsible for X). While a bit passive-aggressive, it usually jumpstarts a healthy conversation. At the end of the day, most of us are striving to get better, be better, and help bring up those around us to do the same because we know that we need help too. Find the touchpoint, the commonality that you and your peers share, and keep it in your mind while working with them. It is challenging to sound like a jerk when you are coming from a humble, positive place.

Building on Previous Steps

Being a real team player means taking time to make your peers better. This is the force multiplying effect I talked about in Leading Self. That effect, again, means not only are you a top performer, but your actions raise the level of performance around you. It is really difficult to build your team up and get them working on the next level if you are really negative or hindering progress of your teammates. This is also another area where someone sprinting up the corporate ladder at the expense of others may disagree. Your coworkers could, and likely will be your competition for bonuses, promotions, and other opportunities to excel. However, if you are integral to making your team better, you probably will end up outshining your peers in the long run.

Helping your peers get better can take many different forms. I would first recommend you tell them about this book. You can also share other professional development materials with them. One of the things the GLDS team has done through podcasting is spend time discussing professional developmental issues and personal growth with each other. Having similar professional development conversations within your office can take many different forms. I have been in offices with professional development book clubs, whiskey and strategy sessions, or a simple conversation with a coworker on how you could have improved a situation that is occurring in the office.

Tactical Tip #21: Hold a low-threat meeting over coffee, snacks, or drinks to discuss the issues your team is experiencing. Allow the newest member, the oldest member, the lowest ranking member, etc. to have a chance to discuss the good, bad, and ugly they see around the workplace. Force yourself to remain quiet and listen to those around the room. Speak last and genuinely address the ideas and concerns of others.

Studies prove that experiential learning methodologies provide life-long lasting power, so the best way to make your co-workers better is to go through experiences with them. These experiences can be as simple as engaging with them before your boss's staff meetings to ensure you provide a unified effort. If you work in an environment where your production depends on your peer's area of responsibility, like a production floor, talk to them about issues before reporting it to your boss. Go to your boss with solutions as a team.

For example, while working in aircraft maintenance, I had daily meetings to provide status updates on aircraft. Each of the three maintenance squadrons depended heavily on one another, and there were many times where we had the opportunity to throw each other under the bus when things were not going as planned. Instead of doing that in front of supervision, just prior to the meeting, I took time to pull my peers aside and let them know my side of any friction points that may be brought up so we could look like a cohesive team in front of upper management. This did two things – it built trust among my peers and it made leadership more confident that we could handle situations at our level. It also presented an area to provide coaching opportunities to my peers to let them know how I was going to deal with the boss.

Avoid Backstabbing

I want you to succeed. I want you to maximize your potential. There is a temptation to climb the ladder as quickly as possible, and sometimes the fastest way to do that is to make your peers look comparatively worse than you. Honestly, this is a solid short-term approach, but eventually, it will catch up to you. When it does, it will be devastating to your career and your relationships. As mentioned earlier in this book, you want to be a vital part of a winning team, and there is just no possible way to be on a high performing team if there is no trust.

One of the challenges faced is playing the blame game. As a leader, if something fails or a mistake is made on your watch, then it is your responsibility, regardless if you had direct oversight of the situation. As I talked about in "Ownership," you need to take responsibility for everything that happens within the team. The same holds true for peer-to-peer groups. If one of your peers makes a mistake and you have the opportunity to trash their name in front of the boss, but do not, that is a fast way to gain trust. To be successful, you cannot afford to talk negatively about people. It is not constructive for a multitude of reasons and will do nothing but slowly destroy the environment.

Going the Extra Mile to Help

From examining my own life, I can pinpoint those few people who, no matter what the situation was, have always left a good impression. It starts with the mindset. Holding your head up high and bringing your positive mental attitude with you everywhere, regardless of the circumstances, will ensure you are one of those people who leave a lasting positive impression.

Being helpful around the office is one way to go the extra mile and leave a positive impression. It is the little stuff that matters here. It can be as simple as refilling the coffee pot when you take the last cup (even when you know that jerk Bill does not), picking up trash that you did not drop, refilling paper in the printer, or asking your office mates if they want anything before you go on your third Starbucks run of the day. Taking this a step further, when you see a coworker who is having a crappy day, ask how you can help make their day a little easier by giving them an assist on a project or taking something off their plate. This can make a lasting impact.

Going the extra mile may seem like a lot of frivolous effort aimed nowhere near what you are paid to do. These little steps have a cumulative effect at making you someone who sets a positive example within the office, likely leading to a more appealing opinion of who you are as a coworker.

> **Tactical Tip #22**: Remember specific facts about the people around you; write it down in a cheat book if you must. If their son has a 5th birthday party coming up, make it a point to ask about how his birthday went. If Dianne two cubicles over loves a cold brew coffee every day, maybe surprise her and drop one off on her desk without her even knowing. Doing things that let the people around you feel seen will go a long way. For the last time, just don't be weird about it.

Leverage Network

Networking, plain and simple, is communicating with someone else who shares common interests, ideas, morals, thoughts, etc. and then leveraging one another to be mutually beneficial. Networking comes in all shapes and sizes and can be performed over any type of medium. From meeting someone face-to-face at a conference to swapping private messages over Instagram, networking is how the world runs. Take the old adage "It's not *what* you know, it's *who* you know." Sure, you can probably grunt it out and make it without networking, but I would argue that you will have a much easier time being successful, in just about any line of work, if you network.

The key to networking is being an honest broker. Do not tell people that you are someone you are not or that you can provide a service you cannot. If you are just starting, tell them that! You would be surprised how many times I told people about writing this book and the positive feedback received, normally followed by an exchange of contact information and ideas. I once had a friend that would say, "Tell the world what you want to do; you will be surprised who wants to help." The more honestly you can portray your goals and current situation, the more others around you can offer guidance or learn from you.

Though we do not always realize it, the people you want to network with are often equally excited to reciprocate. There are many ways to go about networking and many people are afraid to network due to being too far outside of their comfort zone. I have said it before, nothing amazing happens within your comfort zone! The easiest way to network and get over any fear you have of doing so, is to simply get out there and do it, and accept the occasional rejection or failure. The worst that could happen when you reach out to someone is that they do not respond, or say "please do not contact me," but at least now you tried, and you know. It is better to have tried than to constantly think "what if" for the rest of your life.

Just like the section about getting to know your peers, people love talking about themselves, it is human nature. If you struggle with starting conversations or keeping conversations going, the solution is simple: ask questions. Next time you get stuck in a "the weather has been pretty nice recently" conversation, think of a question you can ask to dig a little more in-depth and get to know the person beyond shallow level conversation. Once you get them into a deeper conversation, it becomes easier to respond by talking about your opinions or thoughts on topics. There have been plenty of times where I have been offered jobs or internships by merely talking to people and identifying our desires in life. If you struggle to get past the daily weather commentary, ask them if they were not at work today, where would they be, and what would they be doing? You will be surprised by how many people will open up.

> **Tactical Tip #23**: Next time you are in a networking situation, make someone feel needed. Ask them for their advice on a topic you are struggling with (or not struggling with, but still want their opinion on). You immediately edify the person you are seeking help from and make them feel important. Knowing that you are looking to them for advice will more than likely open them up to asking you for something later, now that they know you trust them enough to approach them for council.

Building a Coalition
What does all the networking talk have to do with your peers? I previously discussed that your line of work is likely a small world. Your peers become powerful allies in your personal coalition of the willing. Grow these alliances by leveraging your network, including "friends of friends" or "customers of customers." Having a group of

people that at least have the name recognition of who you are can, and will, be beneficial within your field.

> **Tactical Tip #24**: When building a team, or coalition, look to diversify your close network. Surrounding yourself with folks who are technically proficient at the same skills or think similarly to you limits the benefits of the network. Network with those who have different skill sets and will challenge your thoughts and beliefs. Conferences, training events, and professional development seminars are great places to meet new people.

Even a High Performer Won't Have Fans

I was selected to attend Weapons School for maintenance personnel. Only the top few percent of military personnel in select career fields get to attend this rigorous three-month course in Nevada. To top it off, I was the youngest person in my 16-person class. Just being selected for this course was an honor but graduating at the top of my class was the goal. I worked my tail off, became an informal leader in the classroom, and did whatever I could to help the team. The work paid off, and I graduated "Distinguished Graduate." I came back to home station, thinking I was untouchable. I was already ahead of my peers just to get into the course, but to do better than the rest of these high performers, I was on cloud nine.

Shortly after returning, I had a feedback session with my new boss. Prior to becoming my boss, he had been elsewhere in the organization, so he knew who I was. During that feedback session, he told me that I was moving around too much and was not building my technical competency. It was a total blow to my ego and some of the most negative feedback I had ever received. He was not nearly as impressed with me as I was impressed with myself. The piece of humble pie that I was served reminded me that being a top performer does not mean that everyone will think highly of you. You likely will still have haters. Typically, most of these haters are peers. They will not understand why you get the more significant projects, more facetime with the boss, more leeway the few times you do screw up. The best thing you can do is realize that not everyone will like you, and when you are provided that feedback, take the valid parts and make changes in your behavior or performance. Most importantly, do not let the haters get you down. It is important to stay humble and not let the feedback totally inflate or deflate your ego. You can learn something from every part of your life if you look for it, the good times and especially the bad.

Tactical Tip #25: When you come across individuals who you do not mesh with and are certain no friendship will be created, work to find commonalities. Find a way to relate to them, continue to ask them for input, and keep them involved. Remain positive and stay persistent in building the relationship with them, they may surprise you and come around.

A boss has the title, a leader has the people.
- Simon Sinek

Leading Down

Up until this point in the book, I have talked about influencing your boss, your peers, really everything up to leading in a formal leadership position. So, how do you most effectively lead subordinates, or as I call it, lead down? That is what this section of the book will focus on.

I am very passionate about leading. To me, there is no higher honor than to be able to formally lead a group of people. Leading is a special duty but also comes with its fair share of humility. This section will give you tactical tips on how you can improve while leading down. A large portion of leading down will focus on expectations, how to set them, and when to change them. The section will give some tips on how you should behave and how you can set the example and ends with building leaders and training your replacement. Overall, this section helps you set the conditions for an effective and efficient team.

Setting Expectations

As I mentioned earlier in the book, getting expectations from your boss is a vital step and your subordinates deserve the same. It continues to be one of the more important things you do, and providing your subordinates with clear expectations sets the tone and goes a long way. Setting these expectations is not just a one-time deal; you should consistently be setting expectations as you progress through your career. I will break up expectations by initial expectations, which are constant, followed by everyday expectations and adjustments. Recall the lesson in Leading Up about how you asked for expectations, work to ensure your subordinates do not need to question any level of your expectations because you laid them out clearly and concisely.

How do you set expectations? Well, you lay it all out there – you tell people from day one what you expect from them in a very black and white way. It even helps sometimes to write it down for them to reference or share with a new person who possibly missed the initial conversation. It is critical, though, to not just write it and forget it, make sure you provide context to explain precisely your intent. Also, ensure you are keeping expectations consistent among all employees, avoid giving different expectations to members performing the same job. Delivering your expectations face-to-face (or voice-to-voice) provides a level of interaction that goes a long way and lets them know you are both serious and sincere. Besides, it gives them that comfort and environment to ask clarifying questions. If you have never set expectations before and are wondering where to start, think about what you would want to know on day one with a new boss. What kind of questions would you want to be answered? What rules and guidelines would you want to be laid out? What would you want to know to be successful in your position?

Example Expectations:
1. Vacation days must be submitted 15 days in advance.
2. Open Door Policy
3. Zero Tolerance for substance abuse or harassment of any Type
4. Always be on time to meetings, if you show up late you will not be allowed in the meeting.
5. If you send an email with time sensitive information, please follow up with a phone call, not a text message.
6. Items needing approval by Senior VP or higher need to be in First Line Supervisor's inbox by 4 PM two days prior to approval deadline.
7. Cell phones are allowed in meetings unless they become distracting, always on silent.

Another item to consider with setting expectations is they may, and more than likely will, change. As long as the change is addressed and communicated to all of the parties involved, change is not a bad thing. Re-evaluating expectations may be needed as things grow and progress. Change means you are evolving and innovating along the way, which you can then only expect that your expectations, and those of the people around you, will also change. A caution though: much like goal setting, if you change expectations frequently, people will start to question the direction and the intent.

Initial Expectations
Initial expectations include how you want your team to behave with customers, upper management, and stakeholders. Another part of initial expectations is how you want your team to work with one another and how coworkers should be treated, inside or outside of work. These expectations should be universal in most, if not all, work centers. I recommend that these initial expectations are provided to your team early on when getting into your new position

or when welcoming and training a new team member. Additional examples of these expectations are responding to e-mail within a certain amount of time, culture expectations (i.e., inappropriate language), how you expect a person to professionally develop themselves, etc. One way I have found to distribute these expectations effectively is to give a copy to your employees so that they can easily reference as time progresses. This can be via email, printed out, shared Google doc, or countless other mediums available with new technology. These expectations will set the foundations of behavior for your team.

Everyday Expectations
Whether you realize it or not, you likely have expectations for every task that you assign your employees. You have an idea in your head of how the task will be completed, what information will be delivered, and what message will be communicated. Most of the time, your employees will not have that same picture in their minds. When assigning a task or project, remember to ensure you accompany those tasks with expectations. You may think that this stifles creativity, and you do run that risk, however, these expectations are meant more to capture your critical requirements of the product/task. Give your subordinates their left and right limits and then let them operate and see what results they provide. Task them with what you need in a finished product but allow them the creativity to get there by their own means, not by giving them an exact roadmap. Leaving room for innovation and allowing outside the box ideas is where the magic happens.

In the government, there are a lot of reporting requirements and data gathering tasks that get passed down from upper management. These typically do not come with a "this is how we would like to see the information" or clearly laid out expectations, so when the upper management receives the data, it is in different formats. It may not even contain the data that really matters. This routinely causes stress and frustration, both with upper management and individual work centers that submitted the data and wasted precious manpower resources. This is something that can easily happen in your office if expectations are not provided.

> **Tactical Tip #26**: Try meeting with your team in the morning to provide daily expectations in a morning tag-up. Let them know what things you are trying to accomplish that day and a summary of what your vision or critical requirements each of their tasks need to meet. If possible, keep this tag-up short as to limit the effect on morning productivity.

Timely Decisions
Expectations can change depending on deadlines. Just about every team leader experiences the battle of deciding when it is appropriate to give their subordinates the freedom to ask questions and provide feedback on a project or process versus when it is necessary to be directive. In other terms, when to give your team creative control and when to tell them to "shut up and color" (as we love to say in the military). The most significant factor in deciding the appropriate path is timing.

As the leader, if you have a tight deadline, you may not have enough time to discuss and banter about the details of the plan with your team; you simply must "go do" and tell your subordinates to follow suit. Unless the change can be made quickly or the feedback is given immediately, you are tied to the current method until time permits a change. Alternatively, when projects or procedures are ongoing and/or enough time is available to take a moment to receive feedback; it is highly encouraged to do so. Be cautious of the situation that Andy Stanley states, "Leaders who do not listen will soon be surrounded by people with nothing to say." So, this battle is important and it is essential to know when to execute both options.

Telling someone to do something or giving fixed directives is simple; however, the tact used in providing "orders" is an art that should be practiced regularly to maintain proficiency. Each situation is unique, and depending on the situation at hand will change your tact. For example, in the world of aviation, seconds can be the difference between life or death. Pilots and air traffic controllers are trained to be "directive then descriptive" on the radio; that is, give the order first and then give the amplifying reason why. A certain level of trust inherently exists between air traffic controllers and pilots, especially while pilots are flying through the weather. An air traffic controller's radar becomes the pilot's eyes as the controller guides a pilot around terrain and other aircraft in the area. If a pilot becomes spatially disoriented, or "lost," while flying through the clouds, and is headed straight for a mountain, the air traffic controller needs to be directive as they only have seconds to tell the pilot to change his or her course to avoid crashing. They don't have time to give details on why they should move or what kind of mountain it is, they need to tell them to move now, then give the descriptive details later once clear of the danger.

In sports, the same holds true whether it be gaining or losing a second in a race, in a football game, or in the pool where seconds and inches make a big difference. The quarterback on a football team gives specific plays and makes calls on-the-go while examining the defense's formation. There is no time for the wide receiver or running back to have a conversation with the coach and the offensive coordinator about what he or she feels is the right play. The coach and quarterback make the call, and the players execute. Many times, they will circle back later and explain why a call was made and the reasoning behind the decision. This can be extremely important in making the connection for your people and letting them see more of the thought process.

When you do have time to poll your team for solutions, Simon Sinek hits the nail on the head with his book "*Start with Why*" and its main premise of beginning with the why behind your company or actions. Providing space and time for employee input is a baseline most top-performing companies operate from.

Tactical Tip #27: Challenge subordinates to make decisions with limited time so that they can come to understand the pressure that you, as the leader, may be feeling. In the military, obstacle courses are used to simulate this; you can take your team to an offsite at a high-ropes or confidence courses to get a similar experience.

Why do You Have to Act Differently?

As a leader, your role changes from being a member on the team to now the person who has the ultimate responsibility to lead the team. Your name is going to be assigned to the product of your team (affecting your brand), you oversee taking care of those around you, and it goes far beyond just participating. You have probably become a leader in the office by working hard, working long hours, grinding it out, and personally creating significant value for the company. As the saying goes, "what got you here will not get you there." The most efficient leader is a force multiplier, someone who is not only great at their specialty but good at training and bringing up those around them. They build their employees to behave and produce much like they produced as they were climbing the ladder. You want to develop systems, processes, and procedures that survive long after your tenure. You should look to do more than personally add value to the company and strive to create value by training your team to optimize their value. Being the leader of the team is not about you rising to the challenge and succeeding, but rather rising the effort of your subordinates in order for them to succeed as well.

You may be thinking, "what? I should not be creating value for the company and build processes that are survivable without me? Would that not make me disposable to the company?" If you are working for a company that values leadership, the answer is a resounding "No." Keep in mind that everyone is replaceable, even if that may be hard to see and hear. If you succeed enough where you acted as a force multiplier, and you truly worked yourself out of a job to the point you were laid off, your leadership attributes will be valued elsewhere.

As an example, as an Operations Officer of an aircraft maintenance unit, I oversaw 400 personnel dealing with operations and conducting thousands of maintenance actions each month. It was a non-stop, 24-hour operation. Leadership-wise, I had a team of six people working directly for me, and together we managed those previously mentioned maintenance actions. One of my mentors and counterparts was simply great at his job. He had a very similar organization to mine, 24/7 operations, a team that managed the maintenance, and he sure could grind it out. To ensure any mistakes at night were fixed, he would come in at four o'clock in the morning, four hours before our first report in the morning, and for lack of a better phrase, he would clean up his team's mess. He was invaluable to his unit, and every time he could not make it to work or took a vacation, his unit's production took a hit. He developed an organization that would suffer when one person missed a day of work. You may be thinking, is this the best approach? In most cases, no, becoming individual dependent and creating that single point of failure can turn out to be a massive pain in the long run.

I took a different approach. I would provide constant feedback to my employees on their performance, walk through the decisions they made each night, ask them questions, and empowered them to make decisions. I wanted them to learn, grow, and ultimately perform as I would, regardless if I was there or not. I also worked with them to develop systems, processes, and procedures that made the unit successful. After a short time operating in this fashion, the organization ran like a well-oiled machine. The benefit of this is that it freed up time for me to think strategically, it got me out of chasing the crises du jour. I was able to set up even more systems to increase productivity and allowed me to do the analysis that was historically lacking within the office. Most importantly, the unit could survive a day without me being there, and it allowed me an improved work-life harmony.

Tactical Tip #28: Work on giving timely feedback as soon as possible. That person may be going to give the same pitch in another hour or so and it would be nice if they knew something sounded wrong, or they were too monotone, or it just may have been off. Do not wait. It may be hard to do at first but consistently work on giving both positive and critical feedback.

Avoid Micromanagement
If you do not change how you operate when you become the formal leader, there is a possibility of some negative repercussions, one of which is micromanagement. I do not need to reinforce that micromanagement is usually a bad thing when it comes to leadership. However, few leaders micromanage on purpose. Most believe their actions are optimal for the organization. But there are long-term impacts to micromanagement.

Micromanagement can be one of the biggest fears of a leader. In the military officer corps, it plagues people who are great doers. These leaders were promoted due to their success producing products a certain way; they now expect their subordinates to build things that look and feel like what they used to build. I worked in a staff job, and a boss of mine would complain about the products that would come through the office. "They suck," he would say. Rarely would he provide feedback as to why it "sucked." The phrase "no news is good news" is applicable here. If I turn in a product and receive no feedback on it, I assume it must have been a solid product and that they approved of the work. A micromanager will not take the time and energy (and it takes both) to train their subordinates to act and produce to the caliber that meets their expectations. It only takes a few times to return products for your team to understand your thought process as you examine their reports.

Now, returning products for corrections only works if you are consistent in your feedback. I had a boss that was one of the most predictable leaders I have known. He probably had no more than 30 questions in his repertoire that covered most critical details of a situation. With this tactic, he provided consistent feedback, both directly and indirectly. By doing this, he could train someone to think as he thinks within a few occurrences. It was not the prettiest style of feedback, and his "feedback sessions," more times than not, turned into significant emotional events where you knew if you had not met his expectations. His style motivated many followers to gather necessary information he would predictably request to prevent one of his classic "feedback sessions."

Beyond not micromanaging, do not be the crutch for your office. If your team depends on your skills, much like my coworker that came into work at four o'clock, they will use you as a crutch and not grow.

Be the Example

"Lead by example." We have all heard the cliché phrase in forums from sports, school, and work. As cliché as it may be, it is one, if not *the* most crucial aspect of being a leader. I believe strongly in this because without having the respect and confidence from your team, you will burn out quickly and your team will get nowhere. If you impose rules and guidelines for your organization, business, office, or whatever group you are leading, for everyone to abide by, you must abide by them as well. It is absolutely vital to set the example and maintain the standard.

A quote commonly told to young military members is, "You are always on parade." I specifically remember it being on the reverse side of the title page of our main Air Force officer handbook. The meaning behind it to a non-military member may be lost at first; however, the message is universal. The quote originates from General Patton. He was writing a letter moments after the D-Day invasion began on June 6, 1944. The letter was to his son, who at the time was a cadet at West Point. Patton was training the Third Army in preparation for upcoming conflict after the invasion of Normandy and, at the time, probably did not realize the lasting impact his letter would have on generations to come. "Always on parade" means that no matter where you are – at the office working hard, at the grocery store shopping, out with friends, or on vacation – you are always being watched and judged by those in your influence. If a member of your team notices you breaking the rules or not following guidance, their respect for you begins to dwindle, and they too feel as if they can break the rules. As a simple example, the military uniform has many guidelines in proper wear. As a leader in the military, if your explicit expectation to your troops is to always wear the uniform correctly, in or out of the office, then you must do the same if you wish to have their respect and expect them to follow your guidance. If a troop sees you at the grocery store after work in uniform but not following the rules, then what do you suppose that troop is going to do? What example are they going to follow? In most cases I have observed, that member will tell others and now the entire office feels as if they too can be relaxed on uniform wear. Furthermore, now that your troops know you do not follow uniform guidance 100% of the time, they will begin to wonder what other rules or guidance you may not follow. This starts a chain of events that never leads to a positive outcome nor builds any type of credibility.

I think you understand the military example, but how does this relate back to the office? Holding yourself to the standards that you laid out in your expectation sessions with your employees is the perfect example. If you asked your subordinate to return emails within a business day, do you do the same? If you told them that it was inappropriate to swear in the office, do you apologize if you let a swear word slip? What about if you have high expectations for timely reporting, do you hold yourself to the same standard when you report to your boss? These are all areas where your employees will know if you are being the example.

Tactical Tip #29: When assigning an expectation or a tasker, stop and ask yourself first if you would do the job and follow the expectations? If you answer no, you should think about what you are requesting.

Provide Feedback –
It's Professional, Not Personal

Have you ever watched yourself on video or when you were speaking in public and wondered, "Why did no one tell me I said 'um' 100 times or why did no one fix my tie that was beyond crooked?" We all have been there and wondered, "why?" Feedback tends to be one of the hardest items for people to handle, whether it be giving or receiving. No one wants to be told that they could do better, that they could dress differently, or that they could have practiced more, but if we never critique one another, we will not know how to get better. It sucks, and it is probably completely outside of your comfort zone, I totally get it – no one wants to be the bad guy. In reality, you are being the better person, and in the end (although it may not be the day your feedback is given) that person may thank you.

Feedback and criticism are all in the way it is handled and the tact that is used. Sure, if you say, "you suck, end of story," the person is likely to not respect you or consider anything you are going to say following that. If you handle it more respectfully, saying, "Hey, have you thought of this, or maybe next time try x, y, or z." People are going to be more receptive and consider your feedback if you come across more humble and genuine with your feedback and critiques. It gets a bit trickier when it is a close acquaintance/friend or even a peer. As previously mentioned, no one wants to be the bad person, but do you want to see a friend or co-worker embarrassing themselves or not performing to their potential? If no one around you is helping them and everyone is choosing to be a bystander, which is common – it has got to be you that provides feedback. Be the person who steps up and helps those around you. Helping make those around you better only helps the team perform better, and that mutual respect grows.

Do not be surprised if that feedback is not accepted whole-heartedly. I will be the first to admit that when I am provided constructive criticism; I hesitate to accept it gracefully. My first reaction is, "Wait a minute, I am usually pretty spot on. Are you saying I am not?" After the feedback sits with me a minute, I usually accept it. For that split second, when it is first heard, I usually get defensive. Do not be surprised if your subordinates or peers react similarly, but just because they reject it at first does not mean it was not the right feedback to give them.

I talked earlier in the Leading Down chapter on ensuring that you set expectations early and correctly, but what do you do when expectations are not met? Do you overlook it and give them another attempt, or do you remove them immediately from the project? The answer that not everyone wants to hear is, "It depends." Usually, if someone is not meeting the expectations that are set forth, you want to correct them as soon as possible. You want to provide the course correction before it gets too far off track. Do not wait until they are a mile down the road to fix their mistake, because by then it could be too late for them to recover. Correct promptly when they take that first step in the wrong direction. Also, try to understand why the mistake was made. Was it blatant negligence or did they potentially misunderstand the expectations that were set? It is essential to discuss the "how we got here," so you can determine where the issues exist and prevent them from happening again.

After expectations are laid out, it is vital to do feedback sessions with your team regardless of how well or poor they are performing. Their initial expectations serve as a baseline, or leveling of the playing field, between your subordinates. They can choose to exceed expectations or completely miss the mark. After some time, where performance was allowed to be measured, it is beneficial to revisit the individual's performance and assess the current state, where they should focus on for self and job improvement and what to continue doing well. At the end of a review period (for example, an annual review), a final sit down is useful to let them know where they ended up and how their performance either set the bar to a new high or fell short. This final meeting would be for the end of year appraisals, bonus reviews, or just yearly feedback sessions. As hard as feedback is, for the most part, people want to know if they are doing well and how they can improve. Be sure to document the feedback and any course corrections. This helps in the long run to justify possible removals or when comparing employees for a potential promotion. You want to see their work history to aid in making an informed decision. In your absence it would also be useful for others to make decisions if there was documentation describing the employees, their work habits, and feedback they have received.

Creating a Team of Do-ers

Legendary Air Force pilot and military theorists Colonel John Boyd, once said, "Do you want to be someone or do something?" His intent was that those who want to be someone, you typically have to be a "company man" meaning someone not willing to upset old processes or challenge upper management. Conversely, a "do-er" was someone always willing to put their career on the line to do what was right for the office or their team. The do-ers would boldly jump into the unknown and would do away with outdated (but trusted) processes in favor of something they felt was better. As a leader, you should strive to support and build a team of do-ers.

If you give your team clear expectations of what their baseline responsibilities are, they should not have any questions on what they need to be accomplishing at work. They can focus their time and energy on creating innovative solutions. In an environment where they are protected from distractions from upper management, they will be freed to spend more time discovering creative solutions to problems and processes. They will have clearly defined bounds to work between and will no longer stress about whether they are responsible for other projects or tasks around the office. They can take their segment of the process or their piece of the bigger picture and say, "Okay, what is happening before my part of the process? What is happening after my part of the process? What do I need to be successful? What does the person after me need from me to be successful?" You can provide prompting to help your employees in their journey to challenge the status quo. Much like I discussed in "Getting Past 'No'," ask them prying questions that challenge their recommended solutions or the burdensome process that frustrates them.

In parallel, stave off the "be someone" careerist mentality. You will, again, be the example. Your subordinates must know you are willing to challenge issues that are accepted by your leadership.

When you have a subordinate that succeeds in breaking an old process, celebrate that success. Gwynn Shotwell, president of SpaceX, a company full of do-ers, said in a speech at a conference full of college students that her team would create epic moments to celebrate. For SpaceX, it was successfully landing an unmanned spacecraft on a launch pad off the coast of Florida after being told numerous times that they could not. Those celebratory, dopamine producing, moments provide cohesion and build worth within the company. In my mind, that celebration is also cementing the do-er mentality within the workforce. In your workplace, these moments may be crushing annual goals or landing a new contract that took months of work to coordinate. Moments that the team all worked together and succeeded together – those are the opportunities to create and push towards.

Building Replacements

One of the most important responsibilities of being a leader is to grow the next generation of leaders. In most cases, you can think of this as building your replacement (being a mentor, a trainer, a guide). For most of us, whether that be in a corporate setting, serving in the military, public service, or just about any job other than self-employment, you will not likely have the option to choose your replacement. Your current supervisor may ask for your input on specific candidates or traits for a successful candidate, but you should not be surprised if you are not included in the hiring process. Furthermore, you may have already moved on to your new position before your replacement takes your position. What all of this means is that you need to leave your team in a good position after your departure. You need to find the people who will carry the baton in your absence so you can breathe easy knowing that your team is in a good place. More likely, however, you need to build up the people around you to take the baton.

> **Tactical Tip #30**: Set up your continuity so that the next person in line has the information they need to be successful. Your important tasks should be at the top of the list. These are the tasks you are directly responsible for completing, reporting, executing, etc., that are time-critical (daily, weekly, or monthly) and that you would consider the foundation of your job. You want to tailor the information so as not to overwhelm your successor. For example, you may not want to go through a detailed list of every single person in your office and share your subjective opinions about them. Instead, what is more useful is to share the list of your go-to subject matter experts for each job, the strong performers on your team, and your employees that have more substantial areas of improvement.

You can help in identifying your replacement by giving employees opportunities to fill in for you. Start with a trial run. I do not advise you to leave cold turkey for a few weeks and use that as your beta test to see if your nominee can keep things afloat. Step out for a meeting or take half a day off with short notice and see how the baton gets picked up and carried forward. Do they succeed, or does production stop?

Take the time to train the potential replacements you are grooming, not just so they can meet the minimum standard, but train to proficiency. Trained and proficient can be two completely different things. Taking the time now, even if it is a little more effort, will, in the end, save you tenfold from having to fix something that was a result of someone not being adequately trained to that proficient level. One of the quotes I learned, practically before I knew how to read was, "If you are going to do something, do it right the first time" – meaning train people to do the job accurately, not cut corners and not half-assed. So many times in life we want the quickest fix. Taking a step back and choosing to spend more time ensuring proficiency, in the end, turns out to be exponentially better. This is an area where I struggle. I would choose to fix my potential replacements work myself because that was the easiest and quickest fix. What I learned to do is take the time to train my replacement to understand and fix the errors encountered even though it takes just a little more time, and then continuing to prepare and practice until at a comfortable level of proficiency.

Training your replacement not only sets your office up for long term success, but it will also provide greater insight for your current employees. As I discussed in the Leading Up chapter, by allowing your potential replacement to see your perspective when they fill in for you, they will learn what they can do to make themself a better employee. This increase in understanding, and the following increase in productivity, will provide you more time to think about strategic issues or even let you unplug from the office, leading to an increase in your work-life harmony.

An additional bonus to having a "full-up" replacement waiting in the wings is that your supervisor will not be afraid to recommend you for a promotion or other opportunity because they can afford to "lose" you and your talents.

Now, what if you are sitting there asking yourself, "What if I am a bad teacher? I cannot train adequately." Well, that is what this book is here for. Take these lessons and learn how to train your replacements. I guarantee there are people within your workplace that you have looked at and thought that they made a great mentor or excelled at taking the time to train and show people around them how to do exactly what they do. Ask those people for help. You are only going to get better if you take the time to be vulnerable, ask for help, and learn. There is no shame in wanting to grow to be a better teacher to help the next group of people coming up in your shoes. It all starts with you putting in the effort to *want* to get better.

Teach Them These Lessons

This book was written to teach, create, and grow influential, successful employees. The best thing you can do as a supervisor or leader is to do just that. This provides a framework, but that is not to say it is the only way to instill these lessons. Now that you have read the lessons and know a bit more about how to lead up, down, across, and self – go teach them to your coworkers, employees, friends, and those around you that are eager to grow.

It all starts with taking care of yourself, or as we described early in the book, as **leading self**. Help others find their definition of success and their "why." Teach them the importance of building their personal brand and the value that comes along with it. Ensure they are practicing for the important moments and perfecting the tips/advice presented. Finally, provide them the roadmap of those first steps they can take without risk. If you have learned something from this book and never share the information, you have failed.

Once you teach the lessons and provide the tools for others to utilize, allow your subordinates to **lead up**. You may not be the lackluster boss we describe throughout the book, but that does not mean you are unable to provide your employee's opportunities to lead you. Make sure you are communicating with your team what is important to you and urge them to communicate on your behalf or prepare correspondence for you to send to upper management or stakeholders. Urge them to ask for your expectations.

Help them become influential among their peer group or **leading across**. Make sure they are helping their peer teammates outside of their direct work center. Encourage them to build and leverage a powerful and diverse network. Watch as they build a coalition of the willing to overcome difficult problems and analyze as they influence their peers directly and indirectly.

Once they are firing on all cylinders, let them supervise so they can **lead down**. Have them set their own expectations of their personnel and stress the importance of them setting the example for their employees to emulate. Watch so they are not becoming a micromanager and stifle those below them. All of these steps will allow the cycle to continue until we all become useful members of the workforce.

Call to Action –
Your Next Steps

So what? What is this all about? Why does it matter if you have influence and become a leader in your workplace or home? Why does it matter if you read books like this and practice their principles? We believe that if you picked this book up or, in the case that someone gave it to you, you went as far as opening it up to see what we have to say, then you have an internal leadership flame within you that is wanting to be fueled. Whether conscious or subconscious, you have a desire to mold yourself into a better version of your current self and become a next-level varsity player. Those are the types of people who can gain the influence of the people around them and pump some positivity into this predominately negative world. That is you! Ready for the good news? You already took the first step. You raised your hand and made a seemingly small decision to read a book that is now, if used consistently, going to pay huge dividends and launch your life on a significantly higher trajectory. If you have not picked up on it yet, we think taking the first step is a pretty big deal, so congrats. Now on to the next step…

This all might sound too good to be true, but let us assure you, we are not here to sugarcoat the process. We are still working on our influence up, down, in, and across every day. It is a process, a grind. The steps are simple, but the application takes trial and error, tact, and time to get right. And after you get them right, getting to a place where your actions are automatic and correct takes even more time, and with that, a lot of failures. The missing piece that we cannot cover for the masses is the great unknown. Everyone's case is different, and it is impossible to write a tactical guide for every possible instance. You might not be in a position to implement all of these tactical tips, or you might have a boss with qualities not discussed in this book that make it impossible even to implement two of them. That is okay! John Maxwell puts it best when he says, "leadership happens daily, not in a day." You are going to have bad days, days where you do not want to go to work. Days where you do not want to practice the important things. Days where you do not want to take your boss's goals and make them your own. If leadership were easy, everyone would be good at it. What is important is that no matter what life throws at you, you keep making forward progress.

As a final note, we want to thank you! Thank you for showing interest in our book and for taking the time out of your schedule to check out what we have to say. We are excited to connect with you and hear what lessons you pulled from the book and whether or not they worked. We love feedback, so please reach out to us and let us know what worked, what did not work, and what you had to tweak to make it work for your situation.

We look forward to hearing from you! And as always...

Good Luck. Don't Suck.

-Dan, Gabbe, and Kevin

www.goodluckdontsuck.com

Instagram: @good_luck_dont_suck | Facebook: @goodluckdontsuck

Tactical Tip Summary

Tactical Tips from
'Overarching Themes of Success'

Tactical Tip #1: Build a goal sheet for your life. My personal goal sheet includes five Sections to emphasize balance: Family, Job/Finances, Health, Education, and Leisure. I start by building Life Goals, then break those down into 10-Year Goals, and further into One-Year, more executable, goals. By breaking goals up this way, it ensures my One-Year goals are consistent and lead to the achieving my long-term goals. When setting goals for yourself, continue to analyze them and revisit them over time. Adapt where needed and tweak them as your path/career changes over time. Change is ok, but make sure you develop smart and measurable goals along the way.

Tactical Tip #2: Find a way to yes. Don't stop at the first "no." If you feel something sounds right, is feasible and legal, find a way to "yes." Do not accept: "No, we can't do that." or "There is no interest" or "That is not going to work," etc. Dig into the naysayer's excuses and find ways to combat them. An easy way to break through excuses is by asking "why?" or when you hear, "We <u>can't</u> do that" instead ask, "How <u>can</u> we do that?". Asking why or how might be all it takes to make breakthroughs on new approaches to solutions.

Tactical Tips from 'Leading Self'

Tactical Tip #3: Find a course that will send the training staff to your office location. This can make it a cheaper option for the office and can allow more of your coworkers to attend.

Tactical Tip #4: Ask a senior co-worker or your HR department about professional development opportunities provided by your company. If none are available, ask if the company will reimburse you for training offered outside of the company. Search for classes that are in line with your profession, possibly provided by the professional organization of your profession. If none, Google search for professional development classes in your area. Another good time to ask about professional development opportunities is during your initial interview and during feedback sessions with your boss or supervisor.

Tactical Tip #5: The Art of Shadowing – When you know you will be out of the office or moving to a different job soon, ensure whoever is going to replace you shadows you for a few days/weeks to really get the full perspective of what you do daily. There are so many little things we do throughout the day that we do not even think about; having someone shadow you through a few days of full processes and operations will let them see everything and give them the opportunity to ask questions when they have them.

Tactical Tip #6: Discuss the next day's schedule with your partner the night before and make sure you both are tracking the same hot items that you/the other need to attend. It may bring to light some conflicts of interest that you now have been able to work out before they blow up tomorrow 15 minutes before the event.

Tactical Tip #7: Identify your "why." Think about your job, your duty, your mission, and ask yourself, "Why? Why do we do it?" One of the best ways to motivate yourself and those around you is to pinpoint your **why** and celebrate it. When you see a victory, highlight it, and celebrate it. If it takes you or any member of your team longer than a split second to answer the question, "Why do you do it?" then you must take massive action to get everyone back on track, including yourself, or you will face failure. Defining your team's "why" early and emphasizing it often will get everyone reading from the same sheet of music right from the start. It will motivate your team in your times of need and bring everyone closer when every factor is working to rip you apart.

Tactical Tip #8: Find the most effective way to practice your craft. You may find the best way to remember a pitch is just by repetition, or maybe it is writing it down over and over, then repeating it over and over. I would also recommend you have someone listen and critique your work. If you will be in a situation where you will be asked questions, build a list of possible questions (better yet, ask others what they would ask you) and be prepared to respond to them.

Tactical Tip #9: If you are running a meeting and notice you are running out of the allotted scheduled time but find you need extra time, ask the attendees if they are ok going over and also allow people to leave if they need to.

Tactical Tip #10: Creating a shared calendar with people in the workplace helps keep one another accountable and setting reminders will keep you ahead of the game. For home life, create a shared calendar with your significant other/family so that you can compile everyone's appointments/meetings in one location.

Tactical Tip #11: Work on physically facing people when you are talking with them and keeping eye contact while talking. Avoid bad habits like fidgeting, looking at your feet, and checking your cell phone or computer while having a conversation.

Tactical Tip #12: If fashion is "not your thing," find an example of an outfit that "fits" your employer's culture on a clothier's website and buy the whole outfit until you become comfortable mixing and matching. Almost as important as what you are wearing, is how it fits you. You are better off buying less expensive clothes and then taking them to a tailor so they fit you properly.

Tactical Tip #13: Google or YouTube search a piece of a project that you have been putting off. You can literally learn how to do anything these days by searching for it online.

Tactical Tips from 'Leading Up'

Tactical Tip #14: Whether you have an extremely competent boss or not, you can still find ways to lighten their load, build credibility, and become a trusted agent. Make the first move and start a conversation with your boss. Let him/her know that you are interested in learning more about [insert work topic(s) here]. Look for ways you can make your boss more successful and take work off their plate. It will give you a chance to shine and make your boss more comfortable delegating work to you in the future.

Tactical Tip #15: Ask your boss for an initial expectation session, regardless of how long you have been in the position. When scheduling this session, provide them a couple of days to think about what they will say and ensure you prepare for what you want to say. Imagine how the conversation is going to go and be prepared to tell them what you expect from them.

Tactical Tip #16: Use calendar reminders (see Time Management under Leading Self). If your boss asks you for an action, put a due date on your calendar when you need to get that information to them. If there is a recurring data requirement, put a recurring reminder. Using your phone calendar works, too.

Tactical Tip #17: When in meetings with your boss, keep a running list of the questions they ask you and others. Write them down and look it over on occasion. You want to recognize the patterns of those questions to help guide what questions you are asking, or what information you think they will want to know.

Tactical Tip #18: Next time your boss has information due, or you need assistance from them, cue something up for them in a Ready to Send email or talking points.

Tactical Tips from 'Leading Across'

Tactical Tip #19: Ask personal questions about your coworkers, write it down and bring up some of the responses in a later conversation. Just don't be weird about it.

Tactical Tip #20: When leading a meeting with peers, take extra precautions to respect their time. Build an agenda with the desired outcomes and distribute it before the start of the meeting. This shows your preparedness and provides you an opportunity to guide the discussion without necessarily out voicing your peers. Again, try not to be weird about it.

Tactical Tip #21: Hold a low-threat meeting over coffee, snacks, or drinks to discuss the issues your team is experiencing. Allow the newest member, the oldest member, the lowest ranking member, etc. to have a chance to discuss the good, bad, and ugly they see around the workplace. Force yourself to remain quiet and listen to those around the room. Speak last and genuinely address the ideas and concerns of others.

Tactical Tip #22: Remember specific facts about the people around you; write it down in a cheat book if you must. If their son has a 5th birthday party coming up, make it a point to ask about how his birthday went. If Dianne two cubicles over loves a cold brew coffee every day, maybe surprise her and drop one off on her desk without her even knowing. Doing things that let the people around you feel seen will go a long way. For the last time, just don't be weird about it.

Tactical Tip #23: Next time you are in a networking situation, make someone feel needed. Ask them for their advice on a topic you are struggling with (or not struggling with, but still want their opinion on). You immediately edify the person you are seeking help from and make them feel important. Knowing that you are looking to them for advice will more than likely open them up to asking you for something later, now that they know you trust them enough to approach them for council.

Tactical Tip #24: When building a team, or coalition, look to diversify your close network. Surrounding yourself with folks who are technically proficient at the same skills or think similarly to you limits the benefits of the network. Network with those who have different skill sets and will challenge your thoughts and beliefs. Conferences, training events, and professional development seminars are great places to meet new people.

Tactical Tip #25: When you come across individuals who you do not mesh with and are certain no friendship will be created, work to find commonalities. Find a way to relate to them, continue to ask them for input, and keep them involved. Remain positive and stay persistent in building the relationship with them, they may surprise you and come around.

Tactical Tips from 'Leading Down'

Tactical Tip #26: Try meeting with your team in the morning to provide daily expectations in a morning tag-up. Let them know what things you are trying to accomplish that day and a summary of what your vision or critical requirements each of their tasks need to meet. If possible, keep this tag-up short as to limit the effect on morning productivity.

Tactical Tip #27: Challenge subordinates to make decisions with limited time so that they can come to understand the pressure that you, as the leader, may be feeling. In the military, obstacle courses are used to simulate this; you can take your team to an offsite at a high-ropes or confidence courses to get a similar experience.

Tactical Tip #28: Work on giving timely feedback as soon as possible. That person may be going to give the same pitch in another hour or so and it would be nice if they knew something sounded wrong, or they were too monotone, or it just may have been off. Do not wait. It may be hard to do at first but consistently work on giving both positive and critical feedback.

Tactical Tip #29: When assigning an expectation or a tasker, stop and ask yourself first if you would do the job and follow the expectations? If you answer no, you should think about what you are requesting.

___

Tactical Tip #30: Set up your continuity so that the next person in line has the information they need to be successful. Your important tasks should be at the top of the list. These are the tasks you are directly responsible for completing, reporting, executing, etc., that are time-critical (daily, weekly, or monthly) and that you would consider the foundation of your job. You want to tailor the information so as not to overwhelm your successor. For example, you may not want to go through a detailed list of every single person in your office and share your subjective opinions about them. Instead, what is more useful is to share the list of your go-to subject matter experts for each job, the strong performers on your team, and your employees that have more substantial areas of improvement.

KEVIN LONG was born in Texas and spent a majority of his childhood in Naperville, Illinois. He attended Auburn University where he received a Bachelors of Science in Industrial and Systems Engineering and his commission as an Officer in the United States Air Force through Air Force Reserve Officer Training Corps (AFROTC). Kevin went on to graduate Euro-NATO Joint Jet Pilot Training and currently flies the A-10 Warthog. He has spent time serving overseas in East Asia and the Middle East and currently resides in Arizona with his wife and fellow Air Force Officer, Ashley.

GABBE KEARNEY was born in New Mexico but grew up for the entirety of her life in Southwest Michigan. She went on to graduate from Michigan State University and the University of Oklahoma with degrees in Political Science and Education. She earned her commission through AFROTC becoming an Aircraft Maintenance Officer on multiple aircraft platforms in the Air Force. Working with the military, extracurricular organizations, and moming a future world traveler have taken her all over the world. She currently resides in North Pole, Alaska with her husband and fellow Air Force Officer Jay and their two daughters.

DAN WHALEN was born in PA but raised for most of his life in Martinsburg, West Virginia. He attended West Virginia University earning a degree in Aerospace Engineering and a Masters of Military Studies from American Military University. Dan earned a commission through AFROTC becoming an Officer in the Air Force and has performed in multiple career fields such as acquisitions, maintenance, and most currently space working for the First Chief of Space Operations of the United States Space Force. He resides in Colorado Springs, Colorado with his wife Alicia.